Keep America Laughing
-at the Left

The Comically Incorrect Cartoons

of

ANTONIO F. BRANCO

VOLUME THREE

THANK YOU!

Your TRUSTED PATRIOT

A.F. BRANCO

Keep America Laughing at the Left
The Comically Incorrect Cartoons of Antonio F. Branco
Volume Three

Published by:

A.F. BRANCO ART
P.O. Box 992
Burlington, WA 98233

ISBN: 978-1-7923-4830-3

Cover and interior layout design: Lovelace9Design, LLC

Printed in the United States of America.

In Dedication

This book I dedicate to all my friends on social media who were instrumental
in any success I have gained in my political cartoon career. You know who you are and I thank you
for your consistent support through all the years.

Thank you to my dear wife, April.
I could not do this if not for your never ending support and friendship.
You are truly a beautiful person inside and out.
I love you dearly.

About the *Author*

U.S. Army 1975 - 1978

"Have pencil, will draw"

A.F. Branco was born and raised in Mendocino County, California, and later relocating to Northwest Washington state.

Branco served in the U.S. Army MP Corps, which offered him the opportunity to attend college on the GI bill.

He is a talented musician — plays guitar, bass, and sings — who, with his band, "Tony and the Tigers," played gigs all over the Northwest.

Over the years Branco created cartoons as a hobby, until he saw America under assault by radical Leftists. Then the hobby became a calling and another form of service to the country he loves and swore to protect from "all enemies foreign and domestic."

Tony's 'toons resonate and inform and do so with razor sharp humor, accruing a following of patriots everywhere.

Branco has appeared on Fox News, the Larry Elder Radio Show, the Lars Larson Radio Show, and more.

A.F. Branco's first book, *Comically Incorrect: A Collection of Politically-Incorrect Comics*, Volume 1 (November 2015), and his second book, *Make America Laugh Again*, Volume 2 (2018), were well received. His calendars sell out each year as the demand for humorous cartoons increases in an otherwise mean-spirited political climate.

And now, with *Keep America Laughing at the Left*, Volume 3, A.F Branco continues slaying the dragons.

Freedom's Battle
by A.F. Branco

Foreword by *Richard Manning*

Tony Branco's cartoons are exactly what political humor has always been – edgy, sometimes uncomfortable but always poignant. Great humor is supposed to not only make you laugh, but also make you think, shake your head at the stupidity described, or even move you to action. Tony's unique ability to make big statements in small spaces truly brings meaning to the old saying that a picture says a thousand words.

As president of Americans for Limited Government, I have been fortunate to be able to work with Tony on producing hundreds of cartoons, many of which are in this book. One thing I can assure readers — Tony cannot spell a lick. In fact, it is rumored that when he was in the eighth grade, he entered an elementary school spelling bee and was eliminated in the first round when he misspelled the word cat.

All kidding aside, Tony's toons are by far the most shared content that we produce and that is a testament to his incredible skill in capturing an outrageous situation in a single drawing, skewering the left like there is no politically correct censorship.

On a personal note, Tony is a genuinely good guy who is a joy to speak with and discuss topics of the day. My wife particularly enjoys when he forgets that he is in a different time zone and calls late at night to discuss a nuance on a toon he is finishing.

But that is his greatest strength, he fights for his ideas and concepts but is open-minded to the very occasional time when improvements are offered. This quality of always seeking the best and funniest line or picture comes through in his work, and I know that you will love this collection that will remind you of spectacularly stupid people and events who could only be involved in the United States political system.

After all, in this time we all need a little laughter, and Tony's cartoons provide much more than that.

Rick Manning

Making America Great

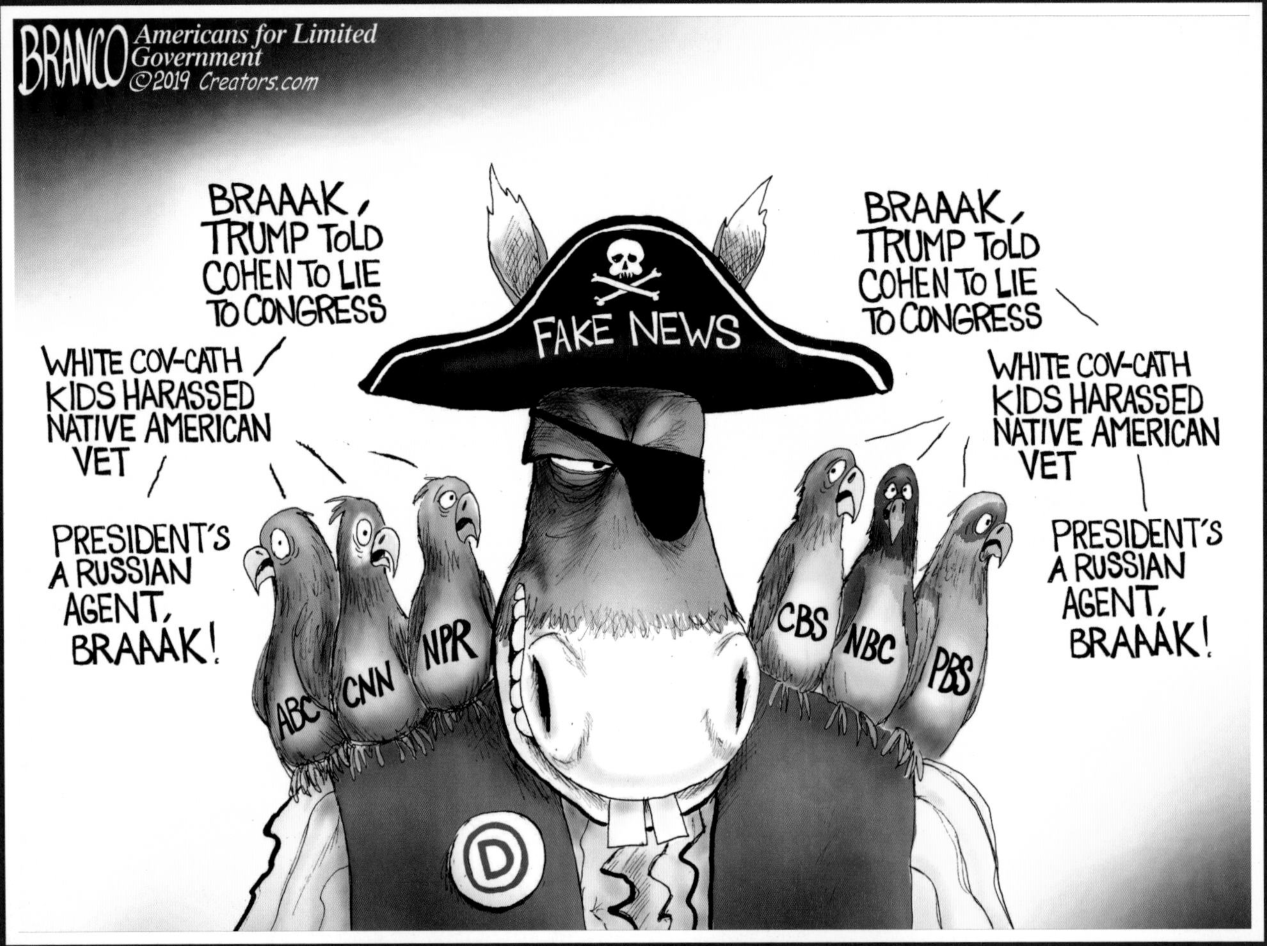

BRANCO Americans for Limited Government ©2019 Creators.com
BRAAAK, TRUMP TOLD COHEN TO LIE TO CONGRESS
WHITE COV-CATH KIDS HARASSED NATIVE AMERICAN VET
PRESIDENT'S A RUSSIAN AGENT, BRAAAK!
ABC
CNN
NPR
FAKE NEWS
CBS
NBC
PBS
D
BRAAAK, TRUMP TOLD COHEN TO LIE TO CONGRESS
WHITE COV-CATH KIDS HARASSED NATIVE AMERICAN VET
PRESIDENT'S A RUSSIAN AGENT, BRAAAK!

BRANCO LegalInsurrection.com
©2019 Creators.com
THAT EXPLAINS WHY SHE THINKS SHE CAN WIN THE PRESIDENCY
ELIZABETH WARREN LIVESTREAMS HERSELF DRINKING BEER

BRANCO FlagAndCross.com
©2019 Creators.com
Email; branco@reagan.com
ROGER STONE
THE NEW FACE OF TYRANNICAL GOVERNMENT OVERREACH

BRANCO Americans for Limited Government
©2019 Creators.com
ROGER STONE ARREST WARRANT
FBI
FBI
FBI
FBI
CNN

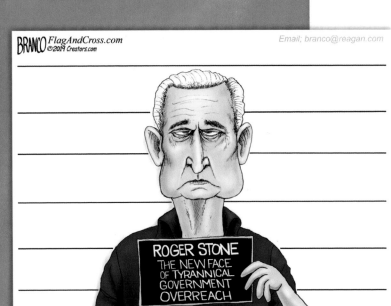

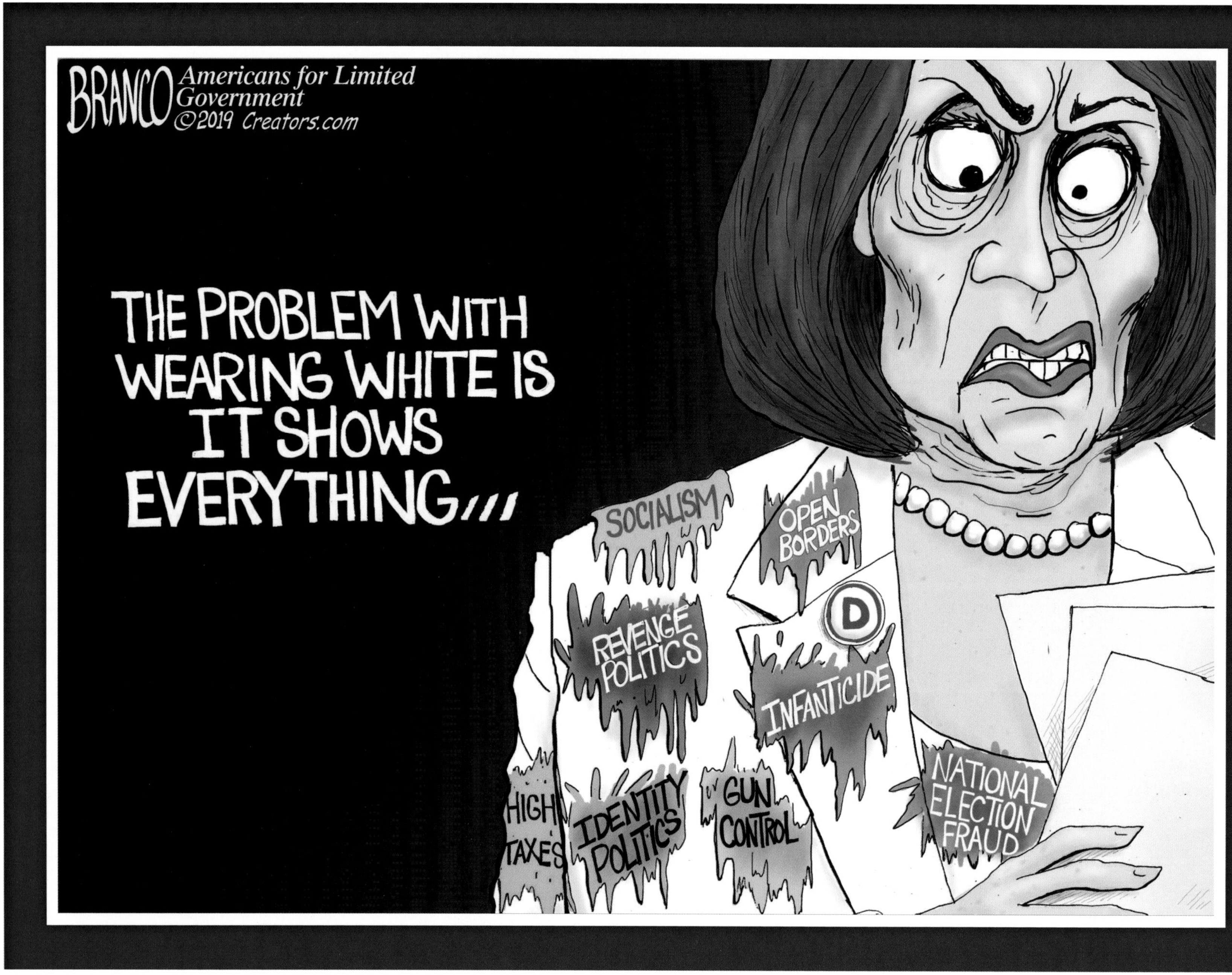
BRANCO Americans for Limited Government ©2019 Creators.com
THE PROBLEM WITH WEARING WHITE IS IT SHOWS EVERYTHING....
SOCIALISM
OPEN BORDERS
D
REVENGE POLITICS
INFANTICIDE
HIGH TAXES
IDENTITY POLITICS
GUN CONTROL
NATIONAL ELECTION FRAUD

BRANCO LegalInsurrection.com ©2019 Creators.com
SINCE WE'RE REMOVING HISTORICAL RELICS OF OPPRESSION, RACISM AND SLAVERY...
DEMOCRAT PARTY

BRANCO Americans for Limited Government ©2019 Creators.com
HOW DO YOU SPELL COLLUSION?
SOCIALISM
ENVIRO-LEFT

BRANCO Americans for Limited Government ©2019 Creators.com
MAGA MELTDOWN
OSCAR

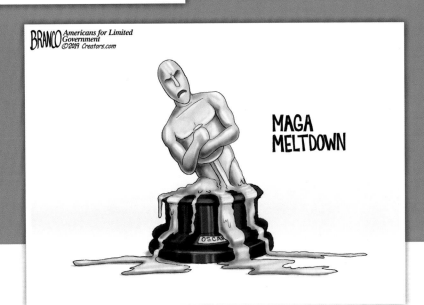

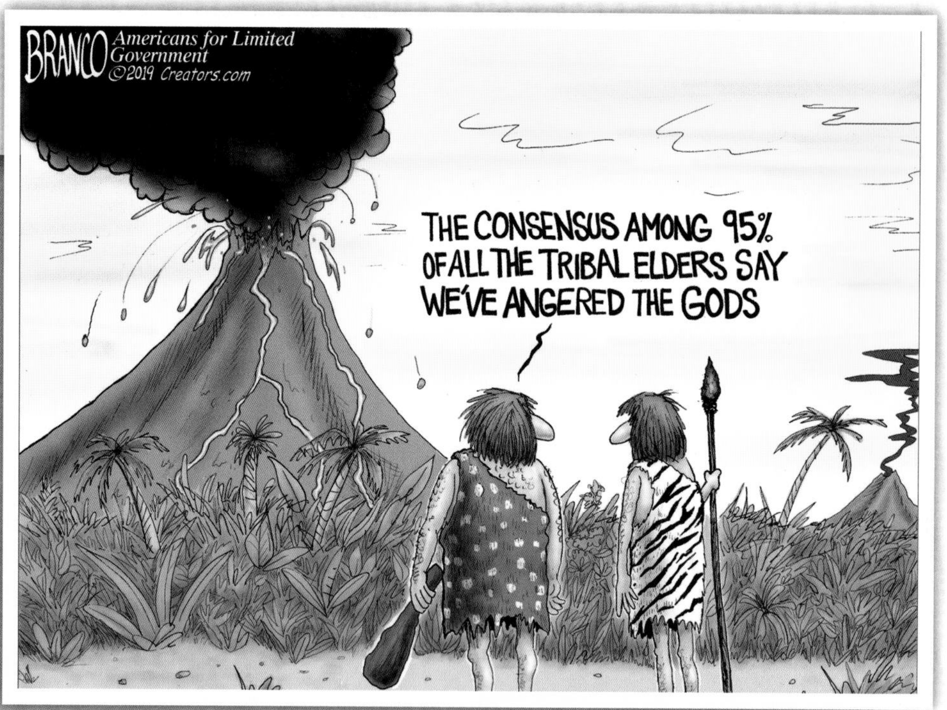
BRANCO Americans for Limited Government ©2019 Creators.com
THE CONSENSUS AMONG 95% OF ALL THE TRIBAL ELDERS SAY WE'VE ANGERED THE GODS

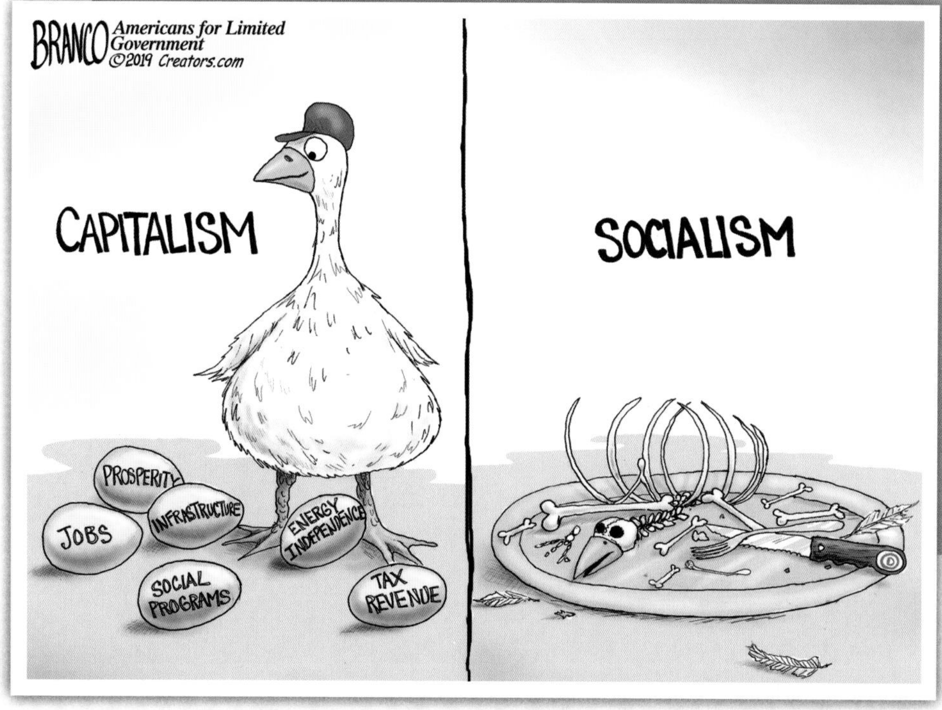
BRANCO Americans for Limited Government ©2019 Creators.com
CAPITALISM
PROSPERITY
JOBS
INFRASTRUCTURE
ENERGY INDEPENDENCE
SOCIAL PROGRAMS
TAX REVENUE
SOCIALISM

BRANCO FlagAndCross.com
©2019 Creators.com
OKAY, YOUR MOVE
GOP
D.C. POLITICS

BRANCO LegalInsurrection.com
©2019 Creators.com
@afbranco
SCHIFF EATING GRIN

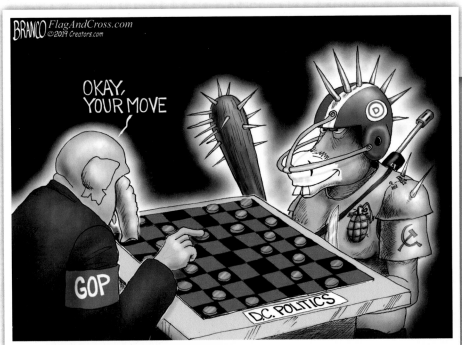

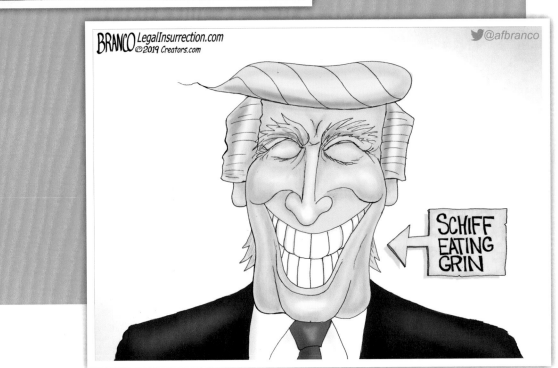

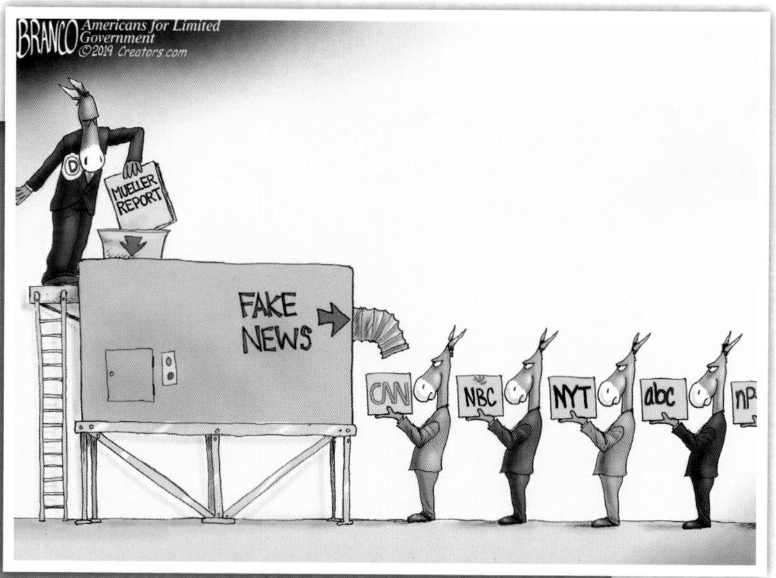
BRANCO Americans for Limited Government
©2019 Creators.com
MUELLER REPORT
FAKE NEWS
CNN
NBC
NYT
abc

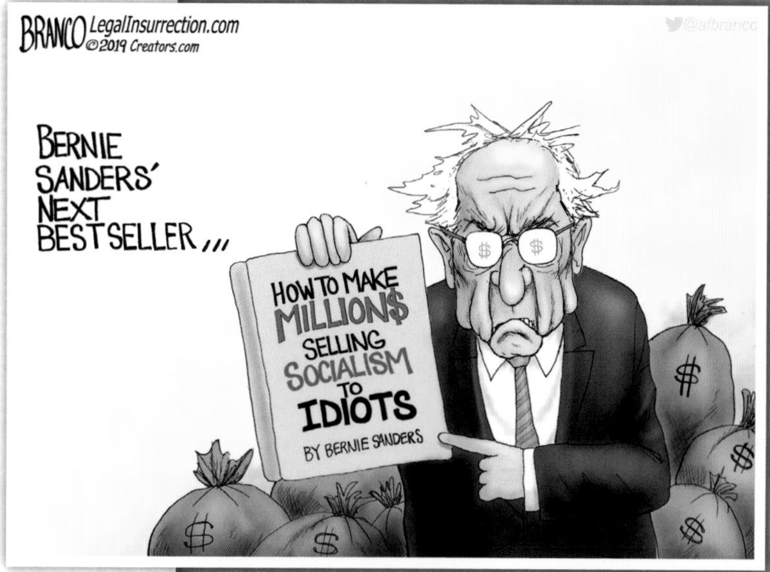
BRANCO LegalInsurrection.com
©2019 Creators.com
@afbranco
BERNIE SANDERS' NEXT BESTSELLER,,,
HOW TO MAKE MILLION$ SELLING SOCIALISM TO IDIOTS
BY BERNIE SANDERS

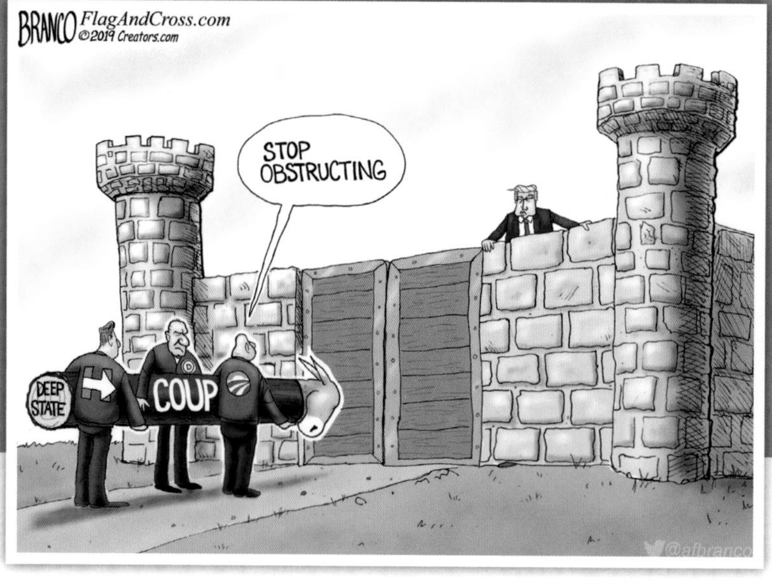
BRANCO FlagAndCross.com
©2019 Creators.com
STOP OBSTRUCTING
DEEP STATE
COUP
@afbranco

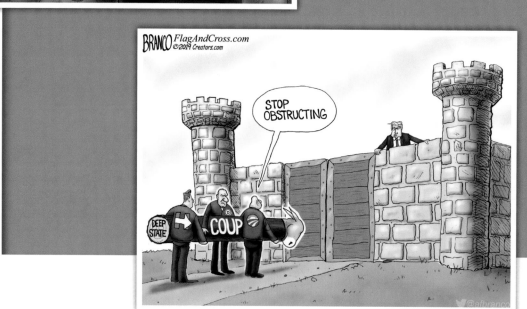

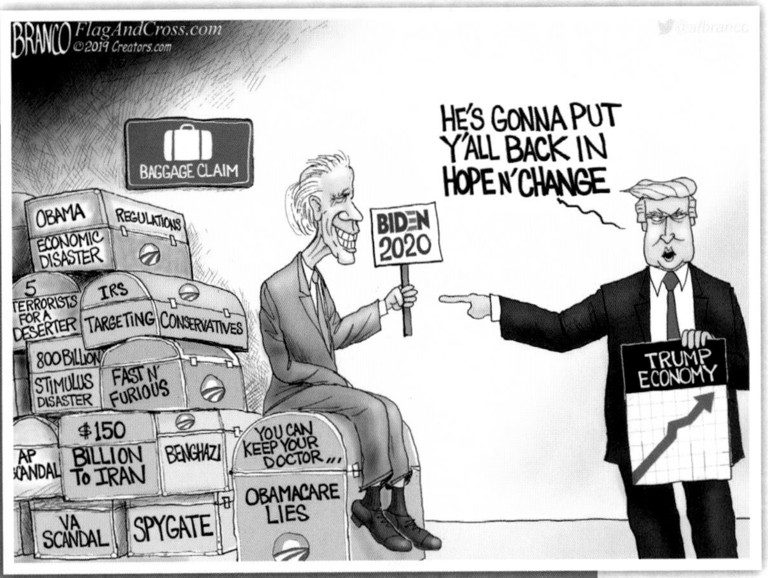
BRANCO FlagAndCross.com
©2019 Creators.com
BAGGAGE CLAIM
OBAMA
REGULATIONS
ECONOMIC DISASTER
5 TERRORISTS FOR A DESERTER
IRS
TARGETING
CONSERVATIVES
800 BILLION
STIMULUS DISASTER
FAST N' FURIOUS
$150 BILLION TO IRAN
BENGHAZI
YOU CAN KEEP YOUR DOCTOR...
OBAMACARE LIES
VA SCANDAL
SPYGATE
BIDEN 2020
HE'S GONNA PUT Y'ALL BACK IN HOPE N'CHANGE
TRUMP ECONOMY

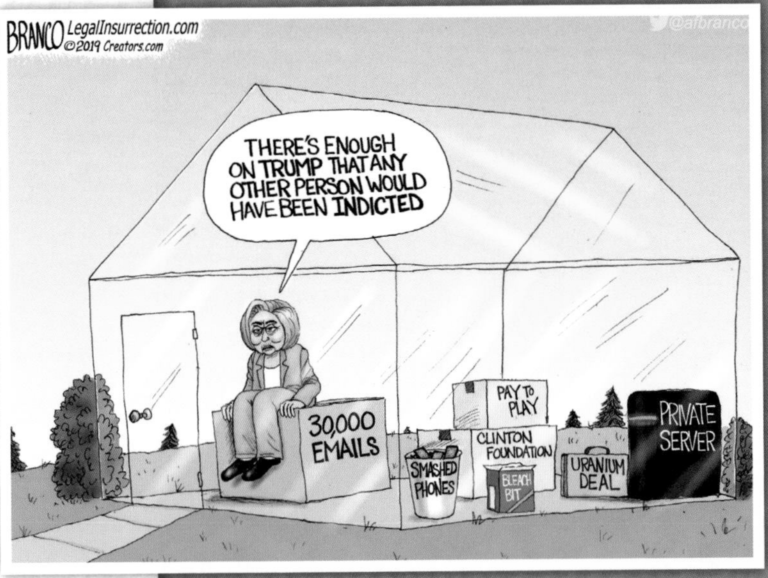
BRANCO LegalInsurrection.com
©2019 Creators.com
THERE'S ENOUGH ON TRUMP THAT ANY OTHER PERSON WOULD HAVE BEEN INDICTED
30,000 EMAILS
PAY TO PLAY
CLINTON FOUNDATION
SMASHED PHONES
BLEACH BIT
URANIUM DEAL
PRIVATE SERVER

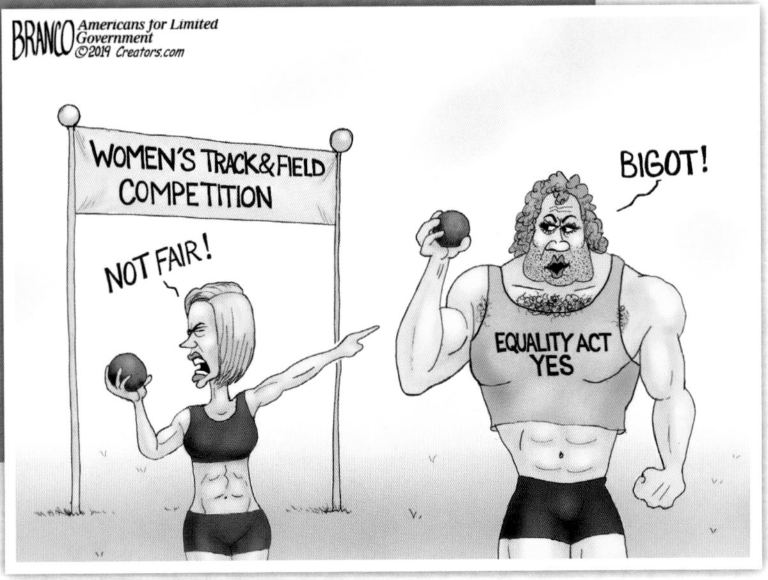
BRANCO Americans for Limited Government
©2019 Creators.com
WOMEN'S TRACK&FIELD COMPETITION
NOT FAIR!
BIGOT!
EQUALITY ACT YES

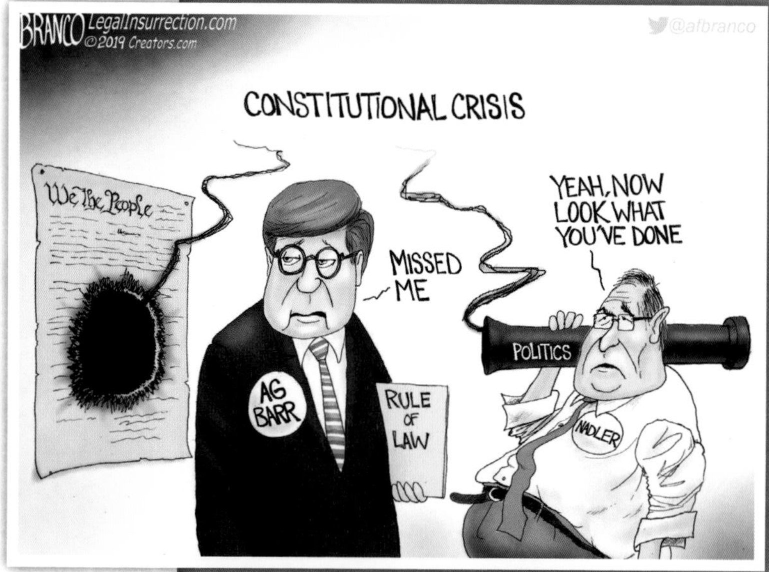
BRANCO LegalInsurrection.com
©2019 Creators.com
@afbranco
CONSTITUTIONAL CRISIS
We the People
MISSED ME
YEAH, NOW LOOK WHAT YOU'VE DONE
POLITICS
AG BARR
RULE OF LAW
NADLER

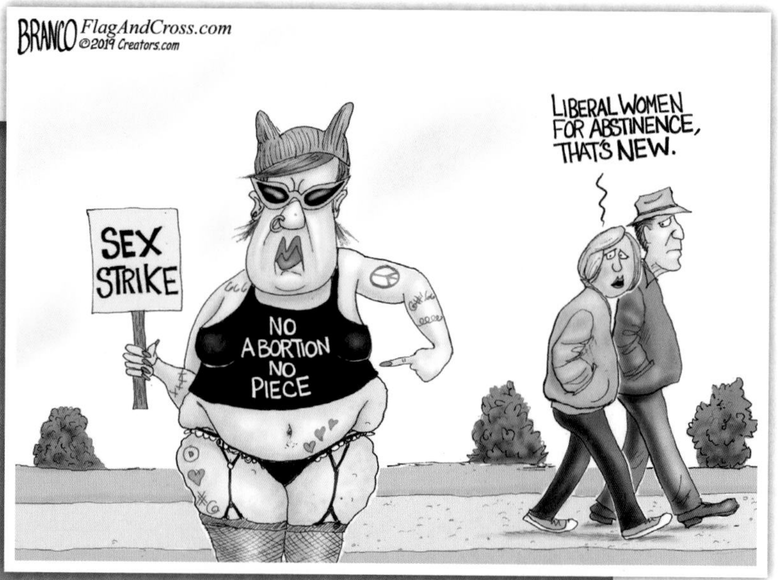
BRANCO FlagAndCross.com
©2019 Creators.com
SEX STRIKE
NO ABORTION NO PIECE
LIBERAL WOMEN FOR ABSTINENCE, THAT'S NEW.

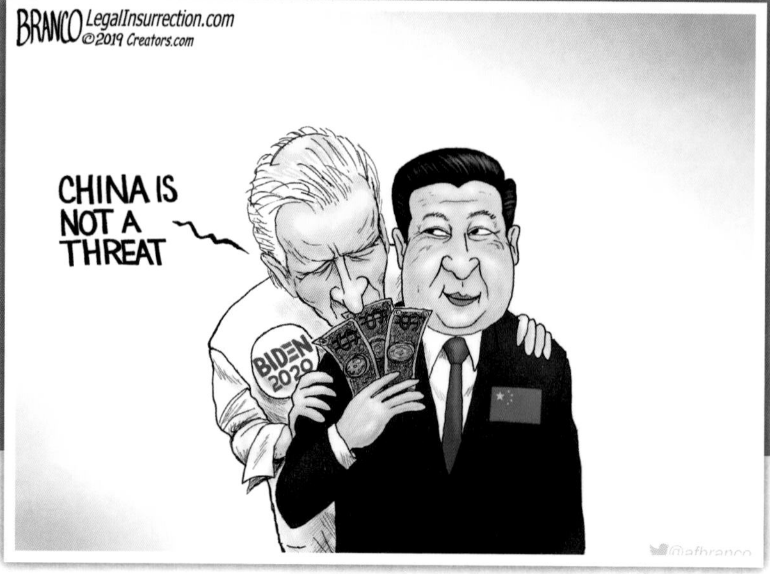
BRANCO LegalInsurrection.com
©2019 Creators.com
CHINA IS NOT A THREAT
BIDEN 2020

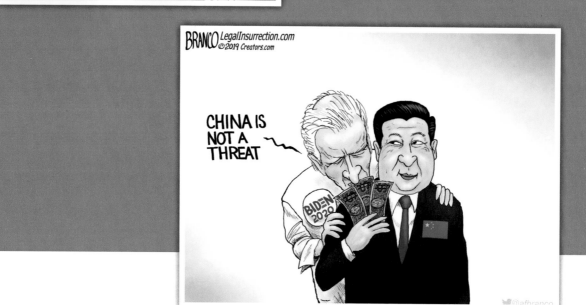

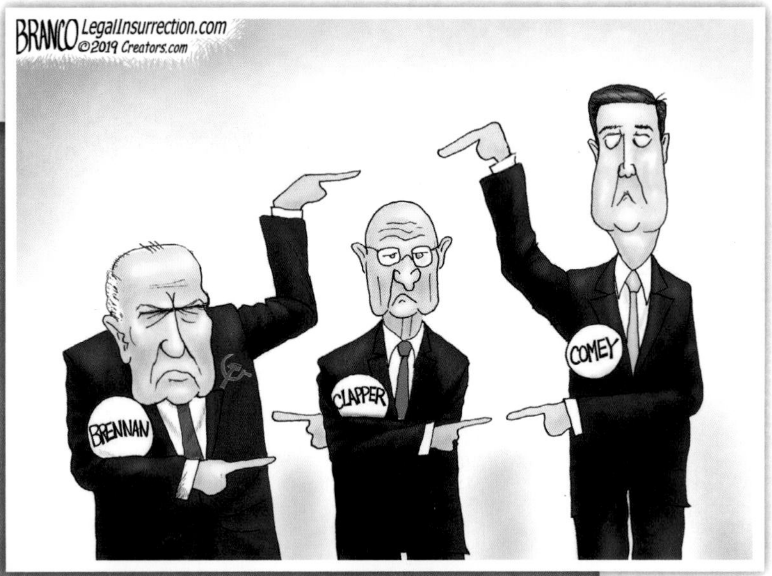
BRANCO LegalInsurrection.com ©2019 Creators.com
BRENNAN
CLAPPER
COMEY

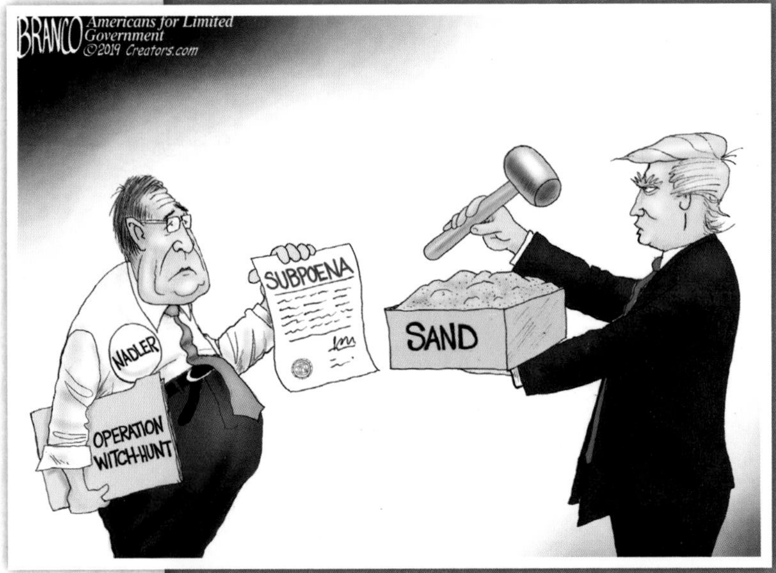
BRANCO Americans for Limited Government ©2019 Creators.com
SUBPOENA
SAND
NADLER
OPERATION WITCH-HUNT

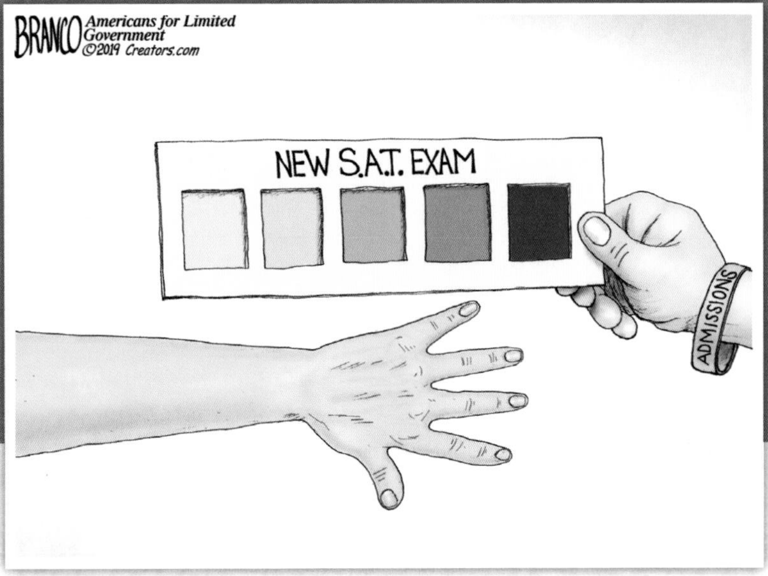
BRANCO Americans for Limited Government ©2019 Creators.com
NEW S.A.T. EXAM
ADMISSIONS

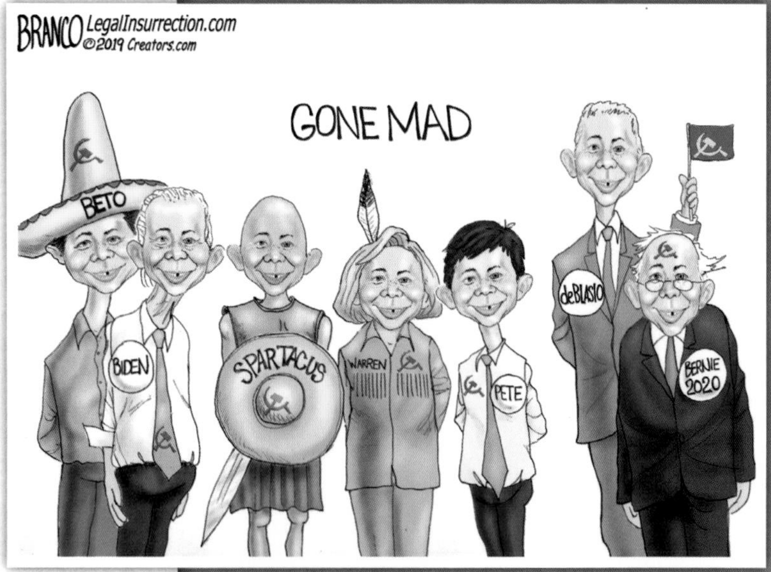
BRANCO LegalInsurrection.com
©2019 Creators.com
GONE MAD
BETO
BIDEN
SPARTACUS
WARREN
PETE
deBLASIO
BERNIE 2020

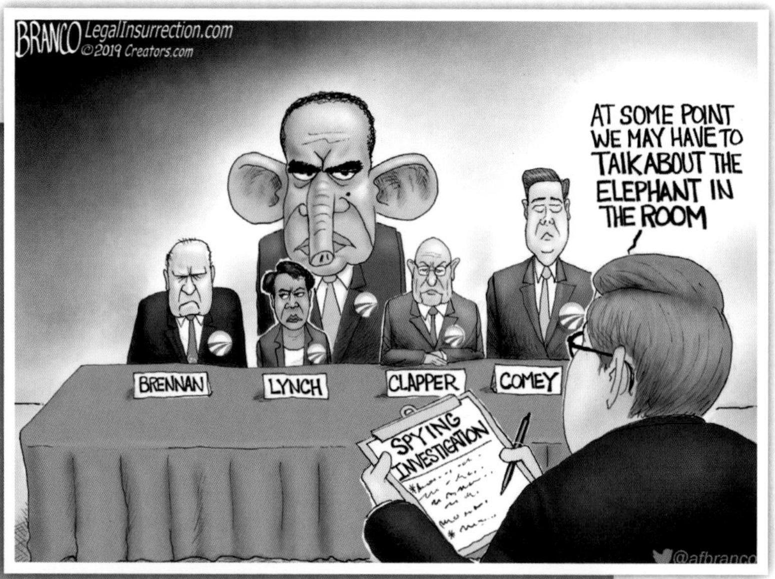
BRANCO LegalInsurrection.com
©2019 Creators.com
AT SOME POINT WE MAY HAVE TO TALK ABOUT THE ELEPHANT IN THE ROOM
BRENNAN
LYNCH
CLAPPER
COMEY
SPYING INVESTIGATION
@afbranco

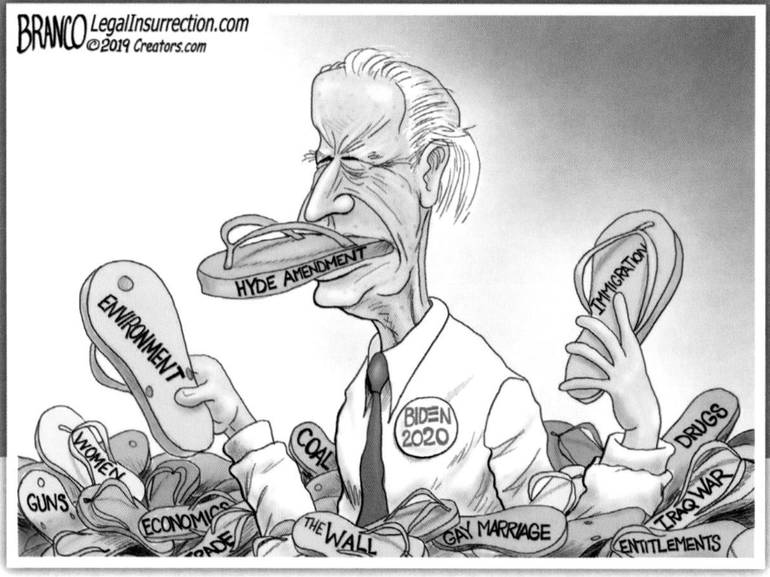
BRANCO LegalInsurrection.com
©2019 Creators.com
HYDE AMENDMENT
ENVIRONMENT
IMMIGRATION
BIDEN 2020
COAL
WOMEN
DRUGS
GUNS
ECONOMICS
THE WALL
GAY MARRIAGE
IRAQ WAR
ENTITLEMENTS

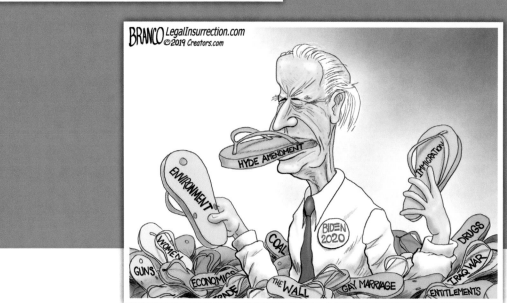

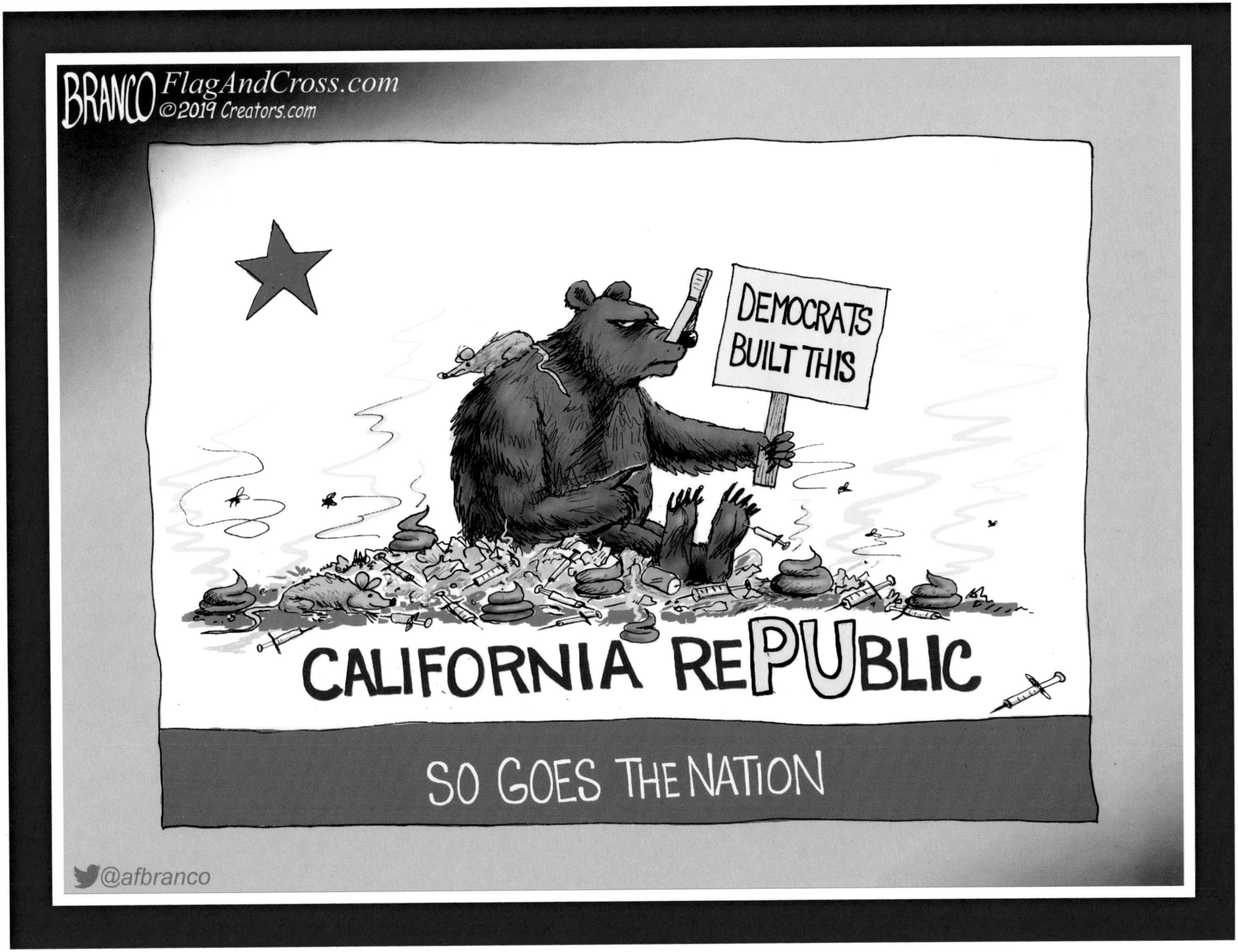
BRANCO FlagAndCross.com
©2019 Creators.com
DEMOCRATS BUILT THIS
CALIFORNIA REPUBLIC
SO GOES THE NATION
@afbranco

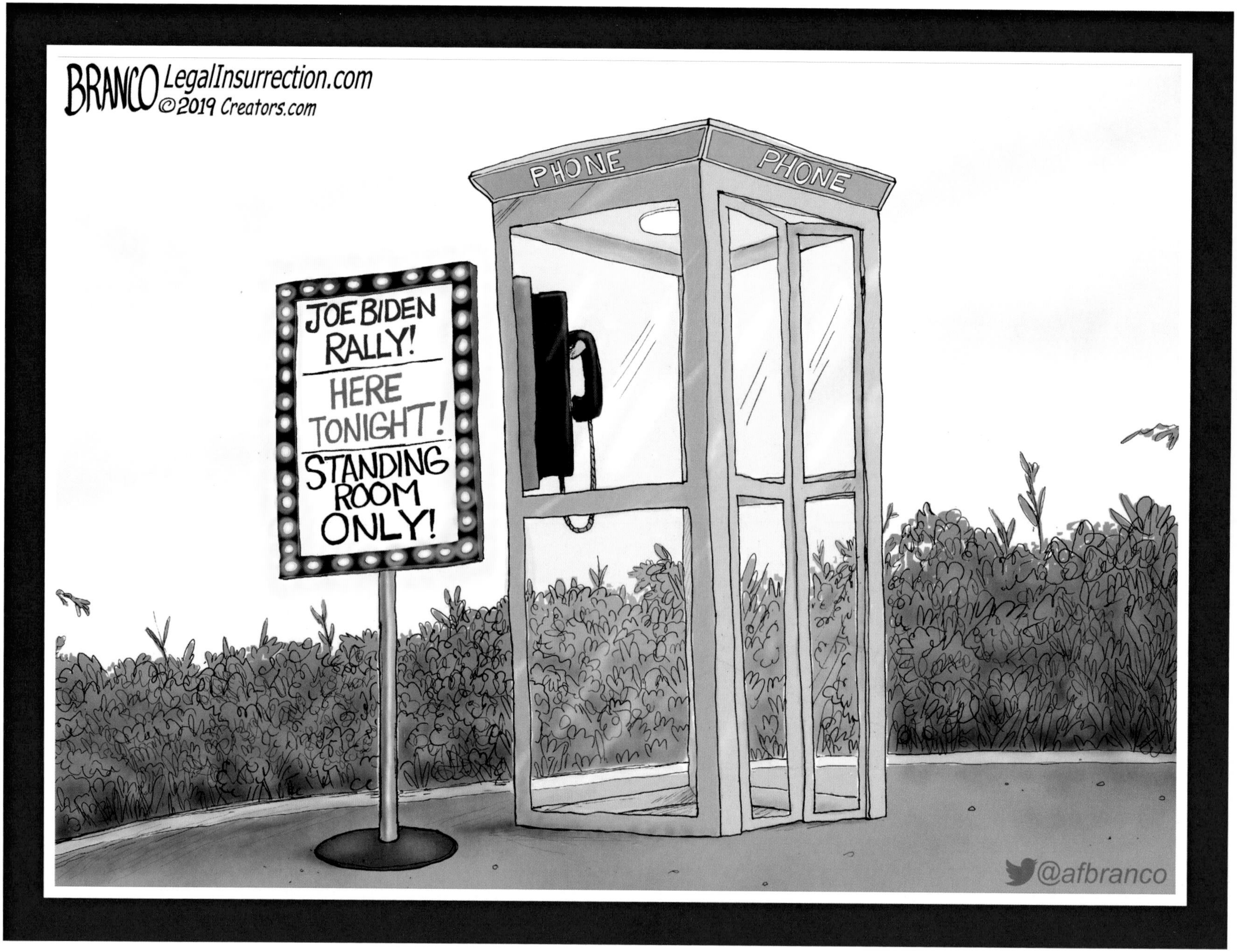
BRANCO LegalInsurrection.com
©2019 Creators.com
PHONE
PHONE
JOE BIDEN RALLY!
HERE TONIGHT!
STANDING ROOM ONLY!
@afbranco

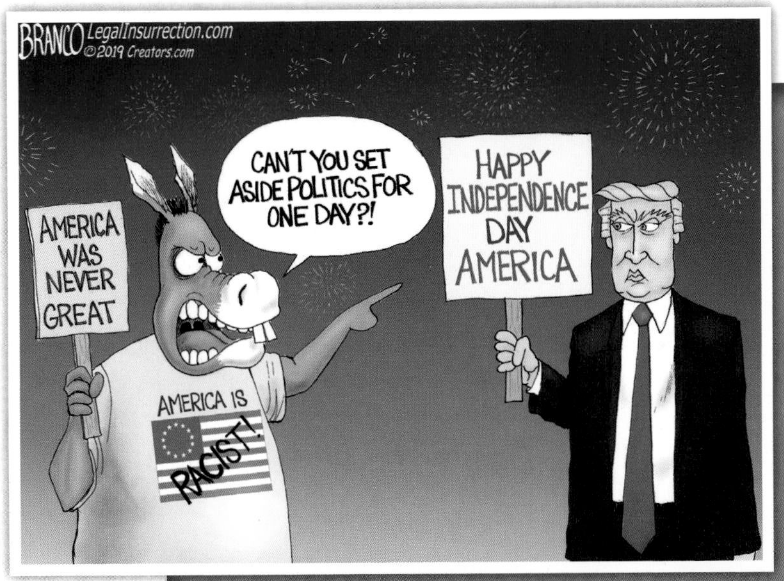
BRANCO LegalInsurrection.com ©2019 Creators.com
AMERICA WAS NEVER GREAT
CAN'T YOU SET ASIDE POLITICS FOR ONE DAY?!
HAPPY INDEPENDENCE DAY AMERICA
AMERICA IS RACIST!

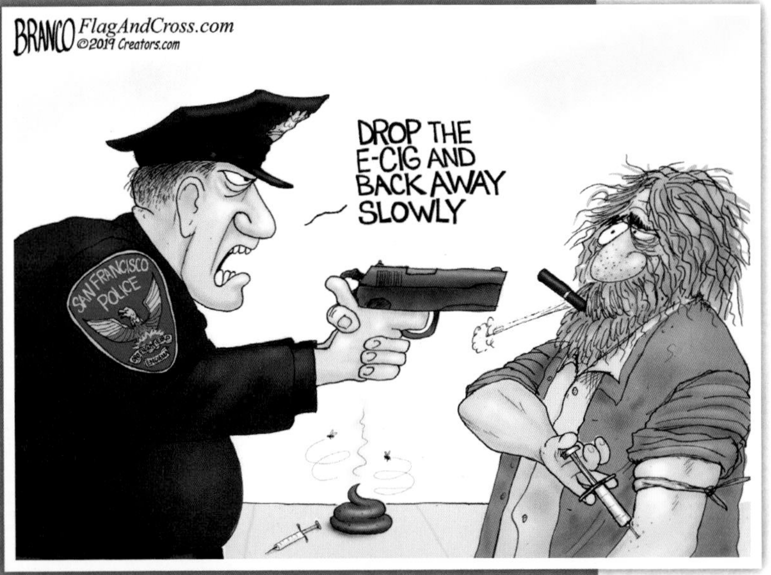
BRANCO FlagAndCross.com ©2019 Creators.com
DROP THE E-CIG AND BACK AWAY SLOWLY
SAN FRANCISCO POLICE

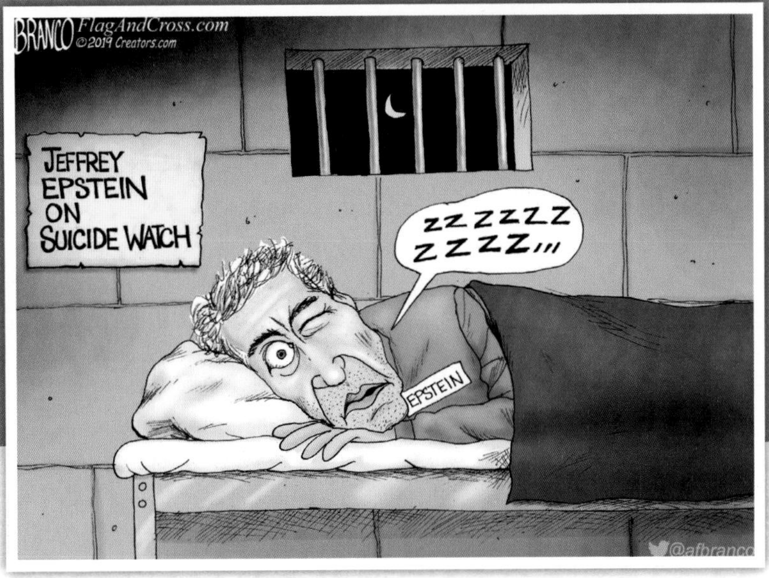
BRANCO FlagAndCross.com ©2019 Creators.com
JEFFREY EPSTEIN ON SUICIDE WATCH
ZZZZZZ ZZZZ,,,
EPSTEIN
@afbranco

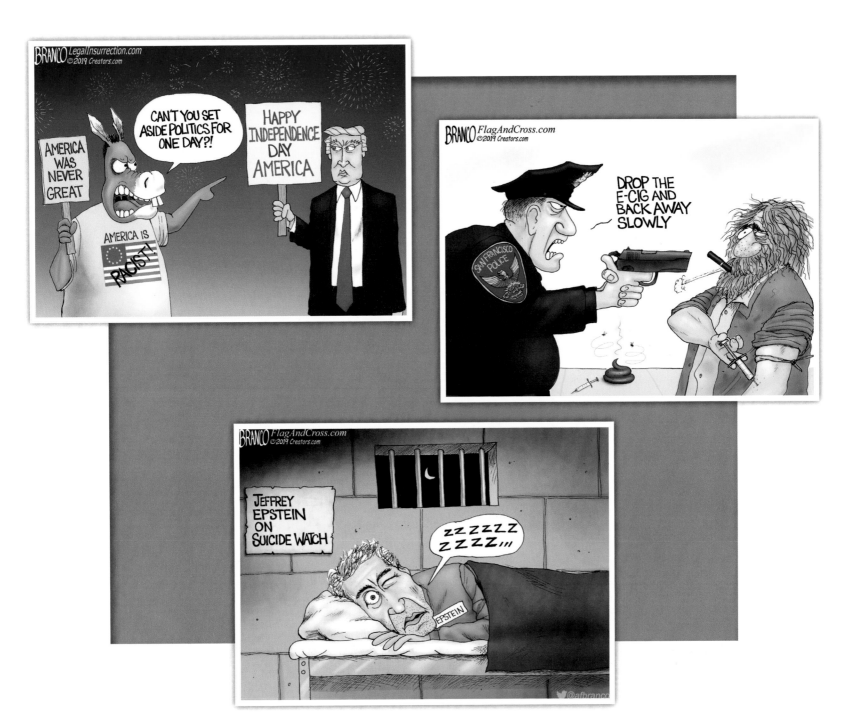

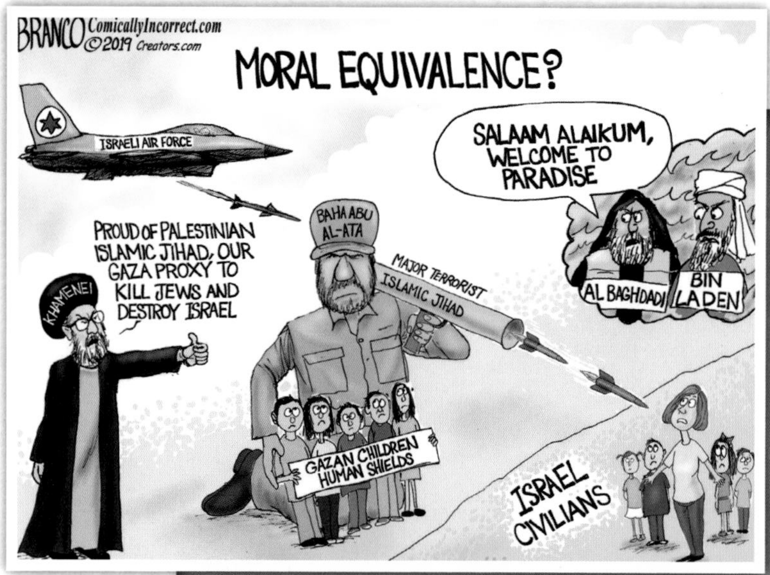
BRANCO ComicallyIncorrect.com ©2019 Creators.com
MORAL EQUIVALENCE?
ISRAELI AIR FORCE
SALAAM ALAIKUM, WELCOME TO PARADISE
PROUD OF PALESTINIAN ISLAMIC JIHAD, OUR GAZA PROXY TO KILL JEWS AND DESTROY ISRAEL
KHAMENEI
BAHA ABU AL-ATA
MAJOR TERRORIST ISLAMIC JIHAD
AL BAGHDADI
BIN LADEN
GAZAN CHILDREN HUMAN SHIELDS
ISRAEL CIVILIANS

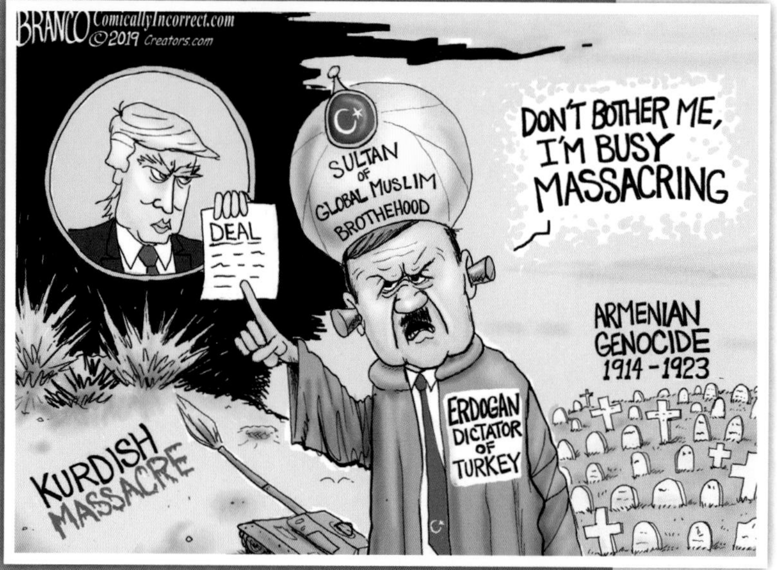
BRANCO ComicallyIncorrect.com ©2019 Creators.com
DON'T BOTHER ME, I'M BUSY MASSACRING
SULTAN OF GLOBAL MUSLIM BROTHERHOOD
DEAL
ARMENIAN GENOCIDE 1914-1923
ERDOGAN DICTATOR OF TURKEY
KURDISH MASSACRE

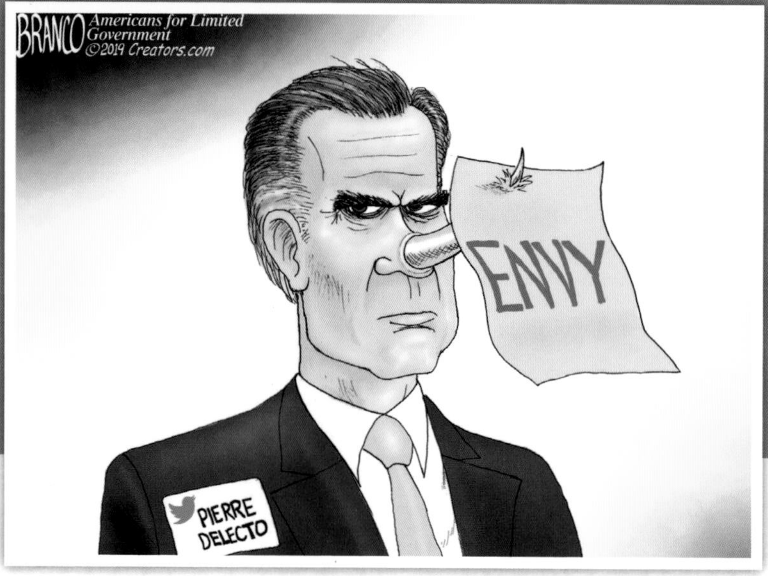
BRANCO Americans for Limited Government ©2019 Creators.com
ENVY
PIERRE DELECTO

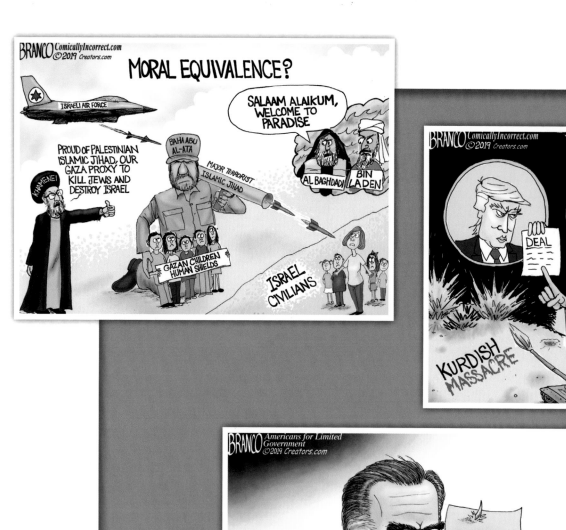

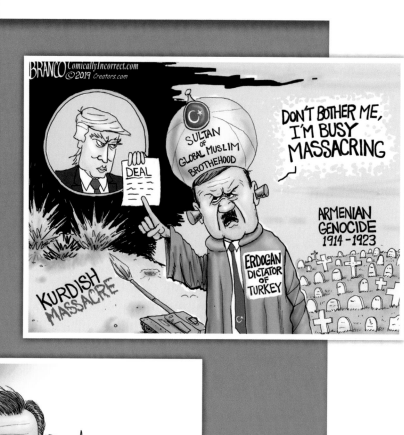

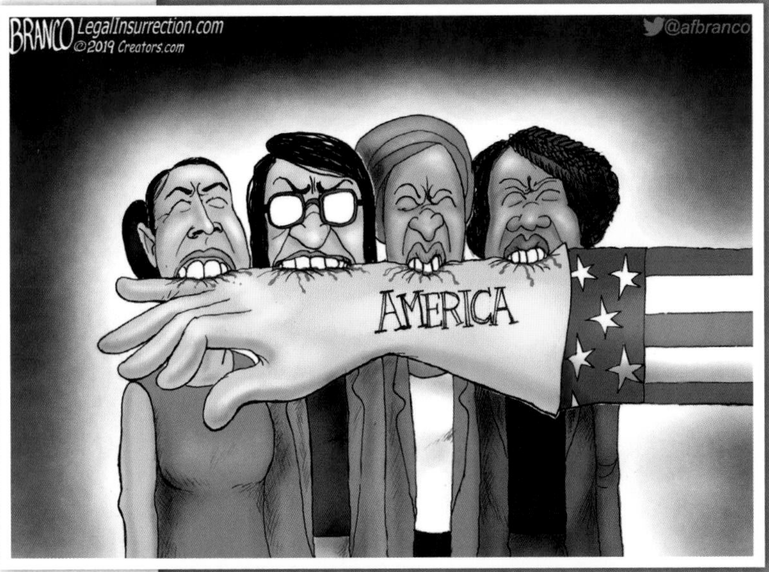
BRANCO LegalInsurrection.com
©2019 Creators.com
@afbranco
AMERICA

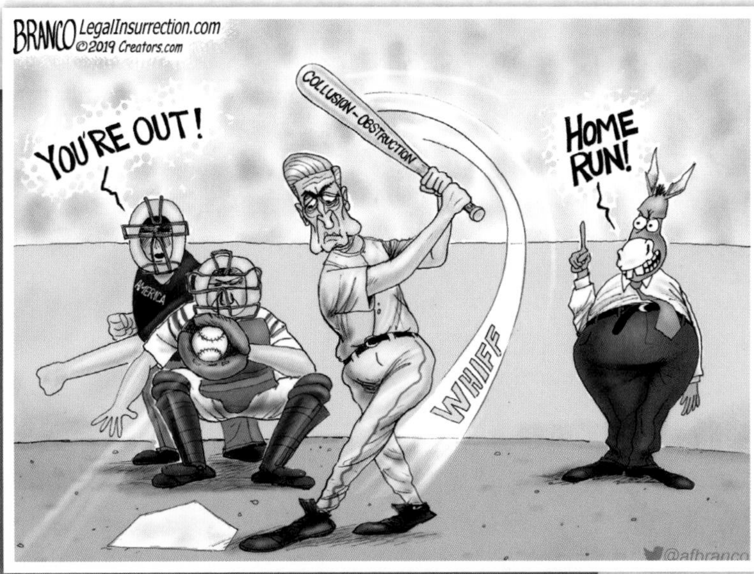
BRANCO LegalInsurrection.com
©2019 Creators.com
YOU'RE OUT!
COLLUSION-OBSTRUCTION
HOME RUN!
AMERICA
WHIFF

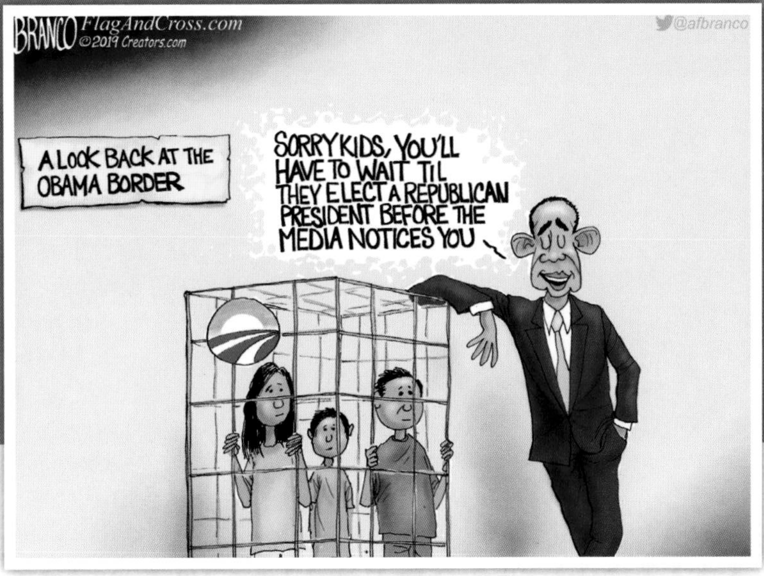
BRANCO FlagAndCross.com
©2019 Creators.com
@afbranco
A LOOK BACK AT THE OBAMA BORDER
SORRY KIDS, YOU'LL HAVE TO WAIT TIL THEY ELECT A REPUBLICAN PRESIDENT BEFORE THE MEDIA NOTICES YOU

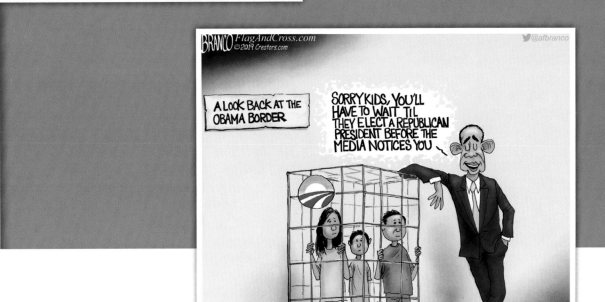

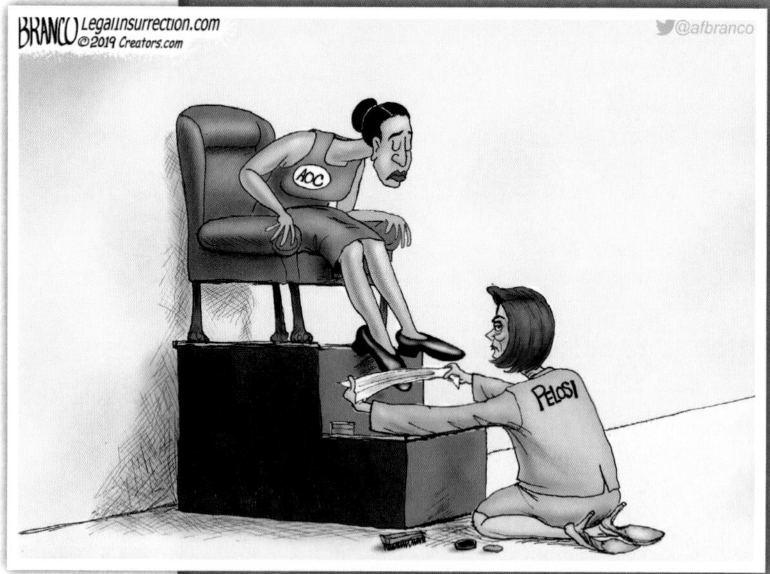
BRANCO LegalInsurrection.com
©2019 Creators.com
@afbranco
AOC
PELOSI

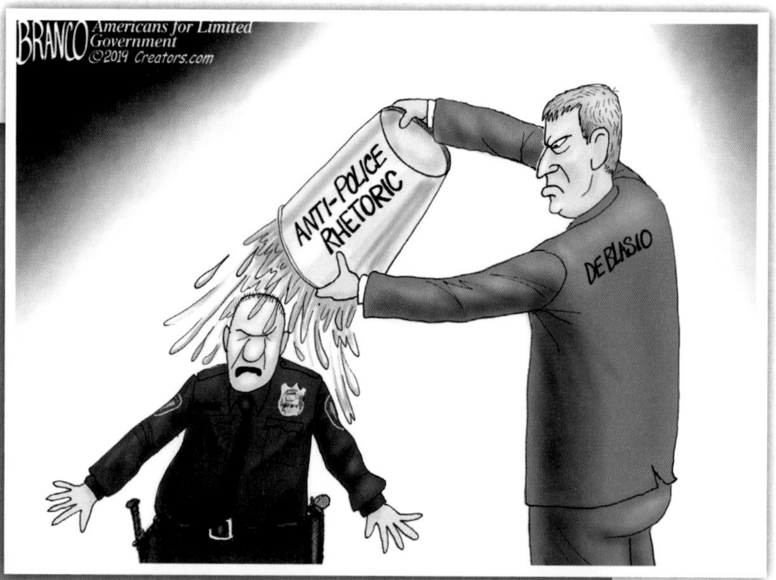
BRANCO Americans for Limited Government
©2019 Creators.com
ANTI-POLICE RHETORIC
DE BLASIO

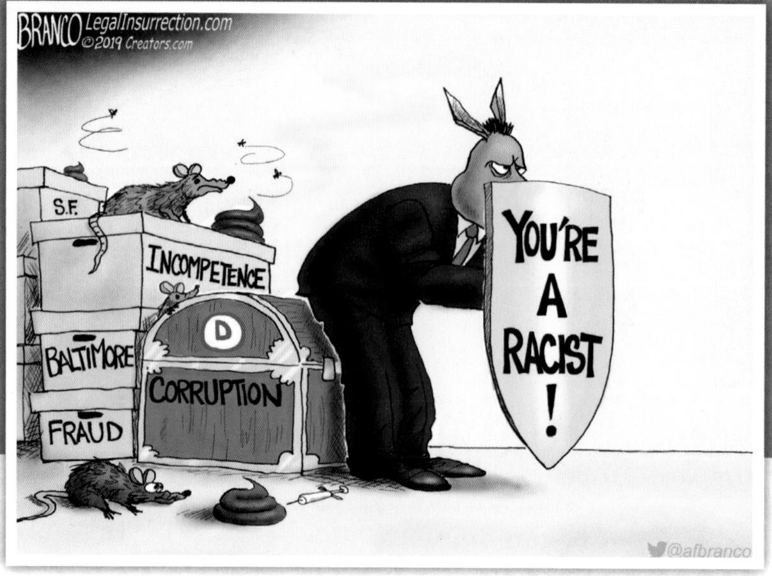
BRANCO LegalInsurrection.com
©2019 Creators.com
S.F.
INCOMPETENCE
D
BALTIMORE
CORRUPTION
FRAUD
YOU'RE A RACIST !
@afbranco

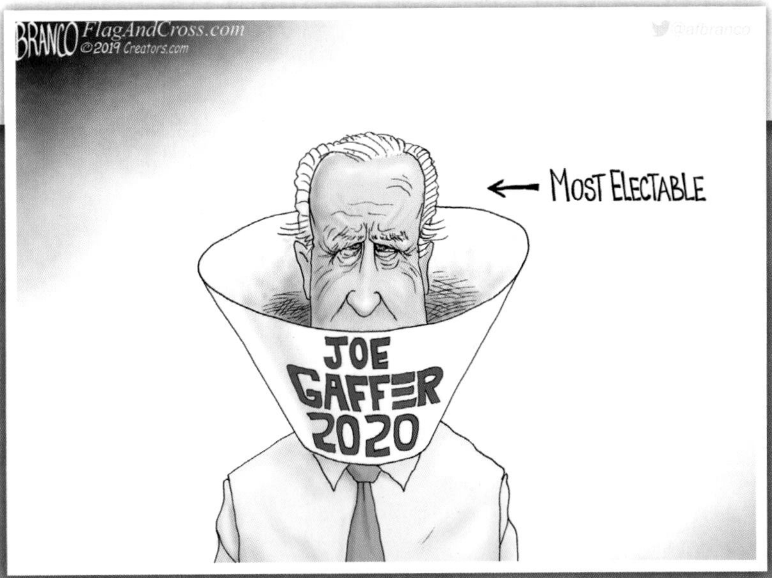
BRANCO FlagAndCross.com
©2019 Creators.com
@afbranco
MOST ELECTABLE
JOE
GAFFER
2020

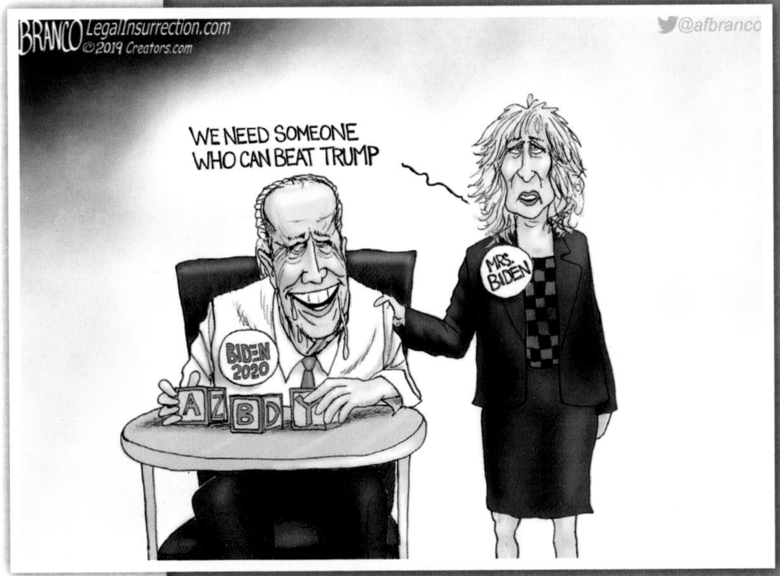
BRANCO LegalInsurrection.com
©2019 Creators.com
@afbranco
WE NEED SOMEONE
WHO CAN BEAT TRUMP
MRS. BIDEN
BIDEN
2020

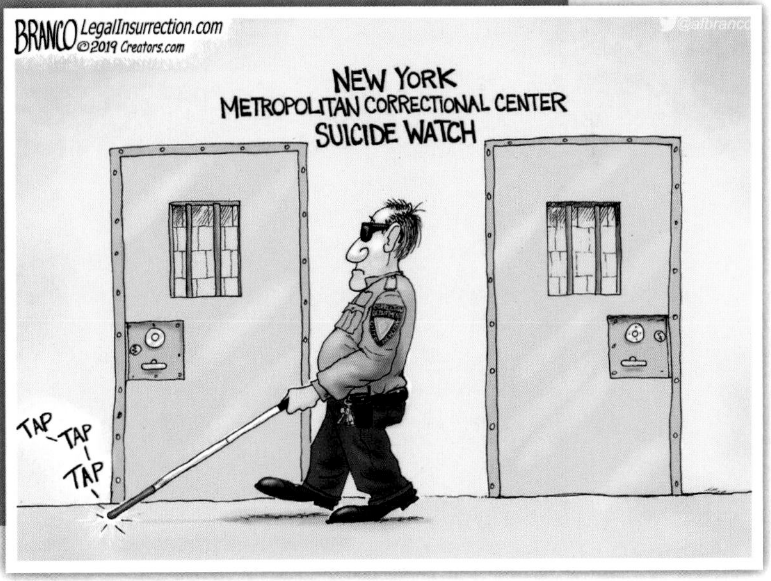
BRANCO LegalInsurrection.com
©2019 Creators.com
@afbranco
NEW YORK
METROPOLITAN CORRECTIONAL CENTER
SUICIDE WATCH
TAP
TAP
TAP

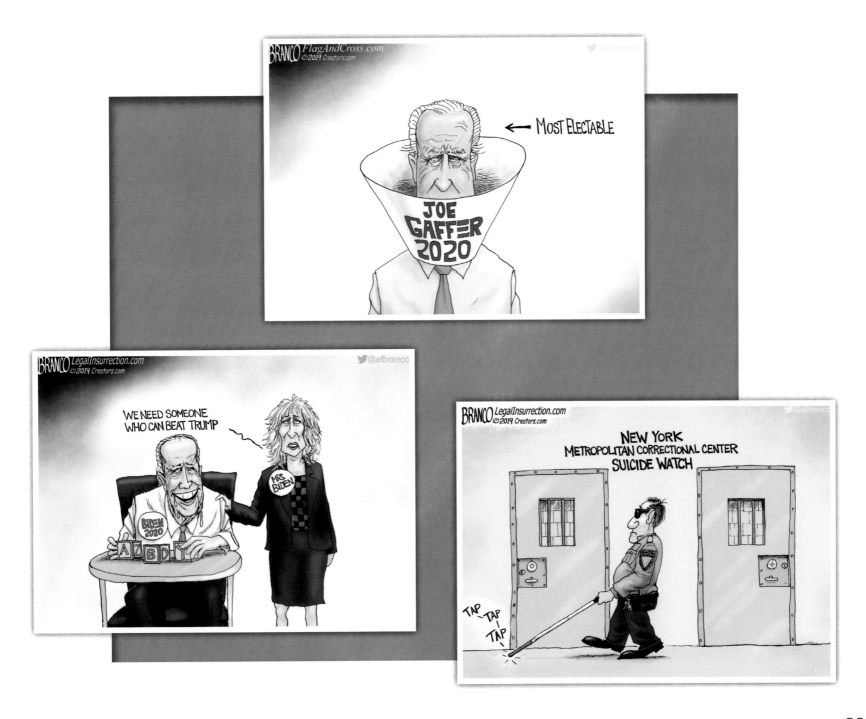

BRANCO FlagAndCross.com ©2019 Creators.com
#@☆*! ROADRUNNER!
ACME
#@☆*! TRUMP
SALE
SALE
OPEN
ACME

BRANCO LegalInsurrection.com ©2019 Creators.com
ARE WE IN BIG TROUBLE DADDY?
DON'T WORRY SON, I'VE GOT THIS.
THE DC SWAMP
HUNTER
BIDEN 2020
MS MEDIA
OPERATION DESTROY TRUMP & BIDEN

BRANCO LegalInsurrection.com ©2019 Creators.com
TRUMP SHAKE-DOWN!
SCHIFF
$$$ UKRAINE $$$
VP BIDEN

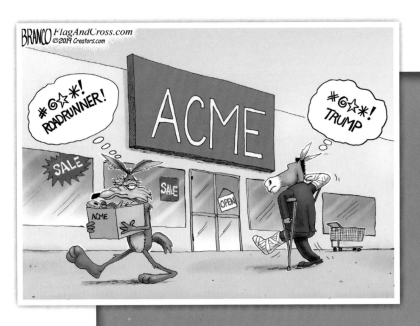

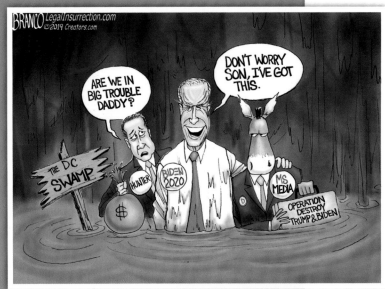

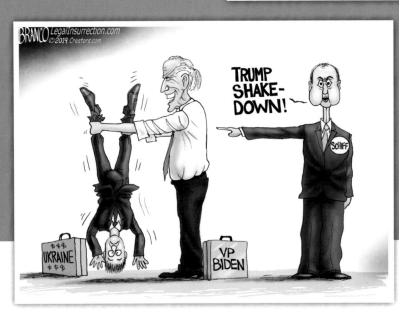

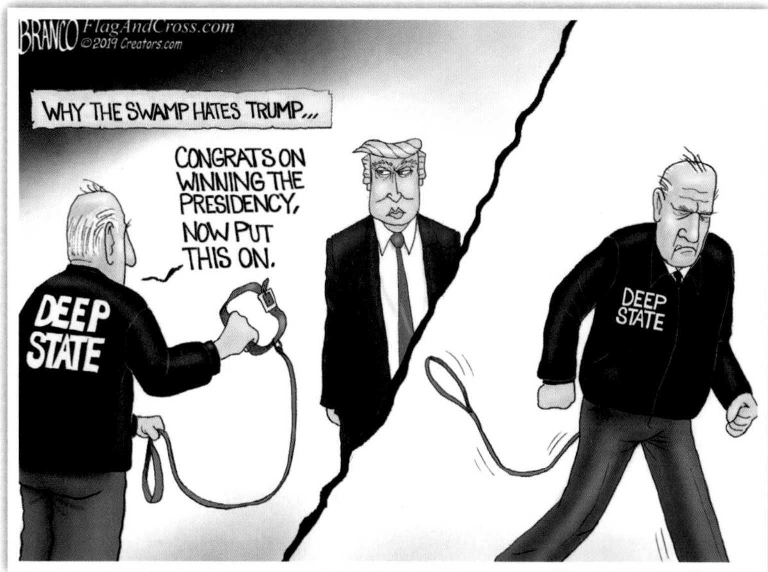
BRANCO FlagAndCross.com
©2019 Creators.com
WHY THE SWAMP HATES TRUMP...
CONGRATS ON WINNING THE PRESIDENCY, NOW PUT THIS ON.
DEEP STATE
DEEP STATE

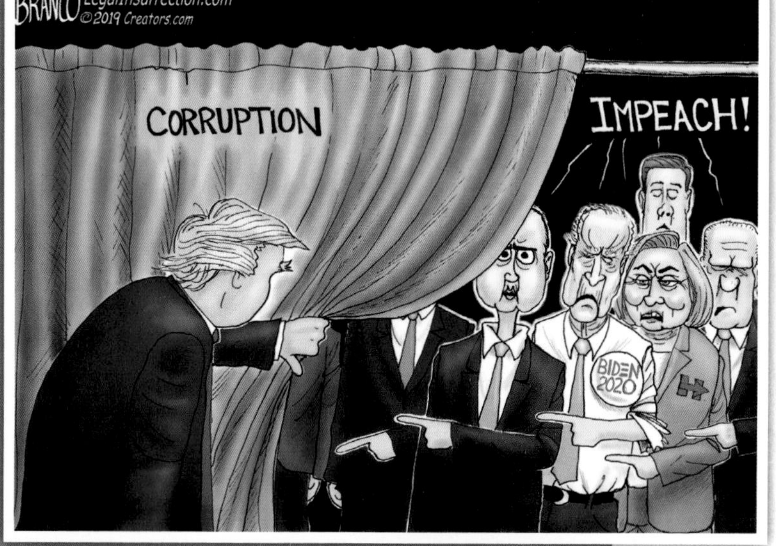
BRANCO LegalInsurrection.com
©2019 Creators.com
CORRUPTION
IMPEACH!
BIDEN 2020

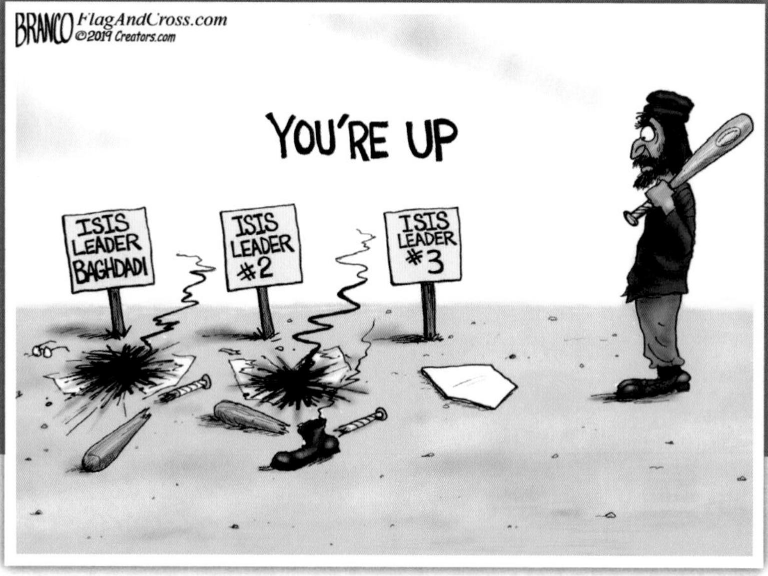
BRANCO FlagAndCross.com
©2019 Creators.com
YOU'RE UP
ISIS LEADER BAGHDADI
ISIS LEADER #2
ISIS LEADER #3

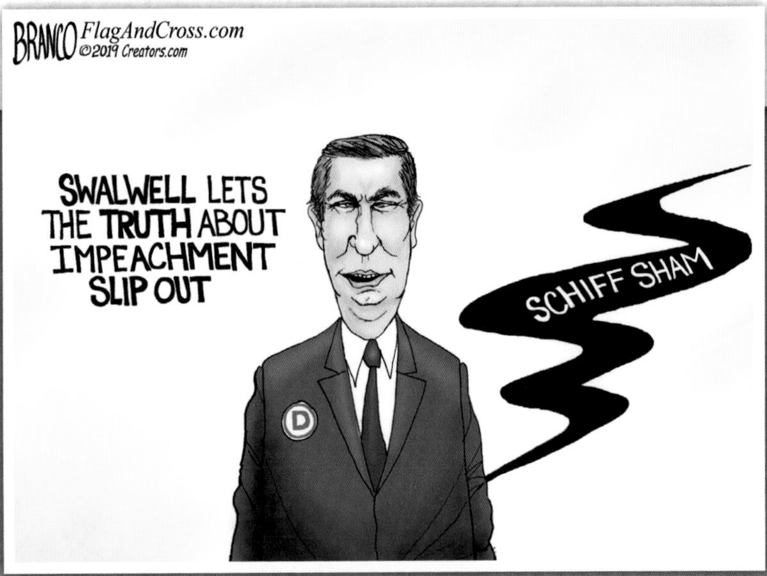
BRANCO FlagAndCross.com ©2019 Creators.com
SWALWELL LETS THE TRUTH ABOUT IMPEACHMENT SLIP OUT
SCHIFF SHAM

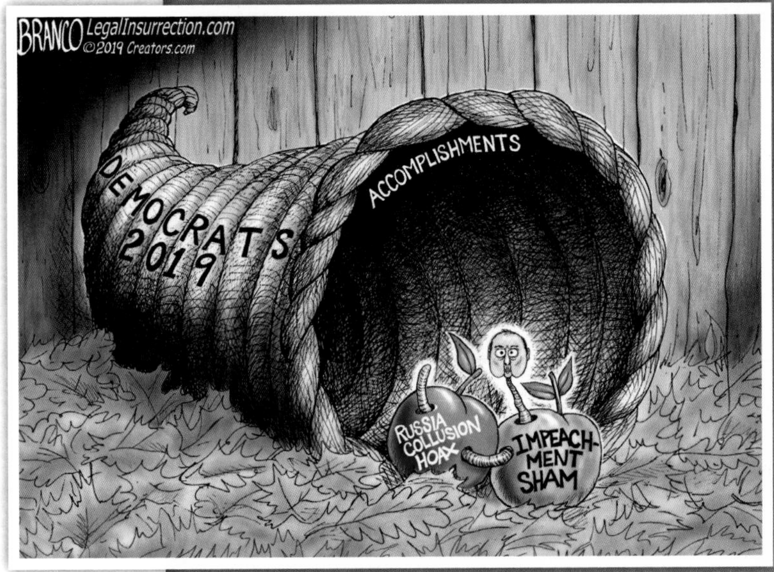
BRANCO LegalInsurrection.com ©2019 Creators.com
DEMOCRATS 2019
ACCOMPLISHMENTS
RUSSIA COLLUSION HOAX
IMPEACH-MENT SHAM

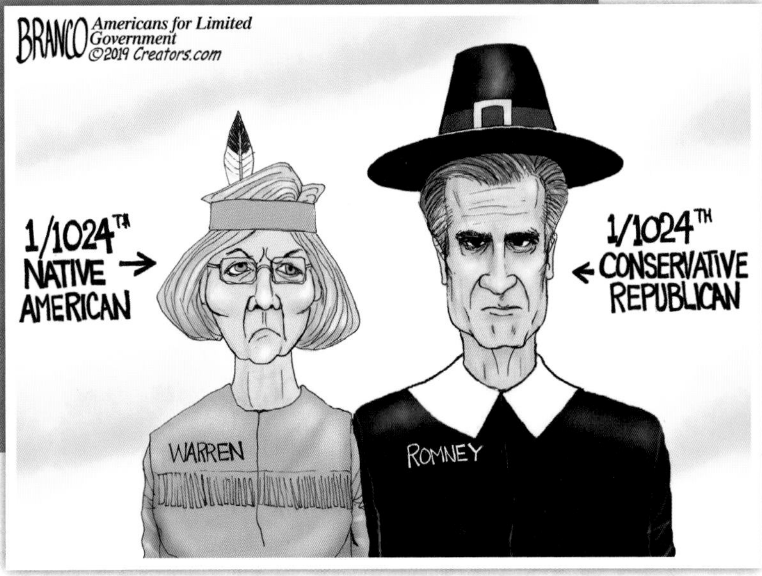
BRANCO Americans for Limited Government ©2019 Creators.com
1/1024TH NATIVE AMERICAN
1/1024TH CONSERVATIVE REPUBLICAN
WARREN
ROMNEY

BRANCO LegalInsurrection.com ©2019 Creators.com
NO INTERVIEWING THE WHISTLEBLOWER!
WHISTLEBLOWER IS OFF LIMITS!
CHICKEN SCHIFF

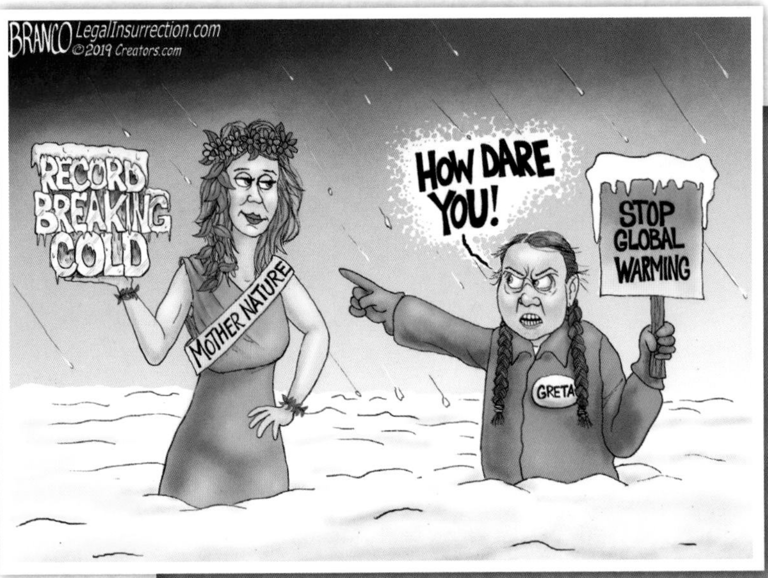
BRANCO LegalInsurrection.com
©2019 Creators.com
RECORD BREAKING COLD
MOTHER NATURE
HOW DARE YOU!
STOP GLOBAL WARMING
GRETA

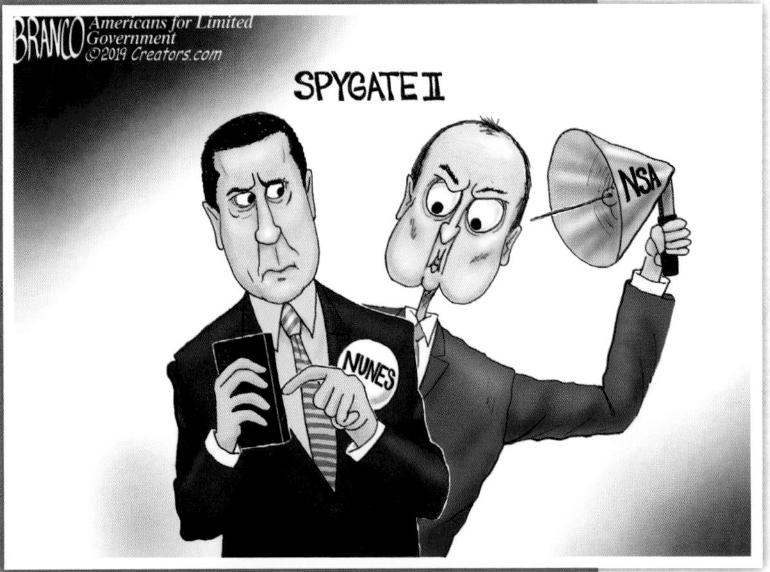
BRANCO Americans for Limited Government
©2019 Creators.com
SPYGATE II
NSA
NUNES

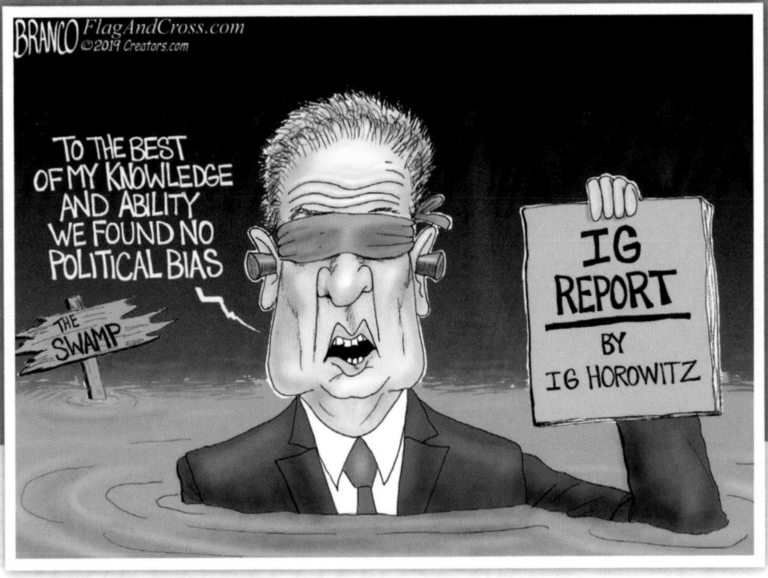
BRANCO FlagAndCross.com
©2019 Creators.com
TO THE BEST OF MY KNOWLEDGE AND ABILITY WE FOUND NO POLITICAL BIAS
THE SWAMP
IG REPORT
BY
IG HOROWITZ

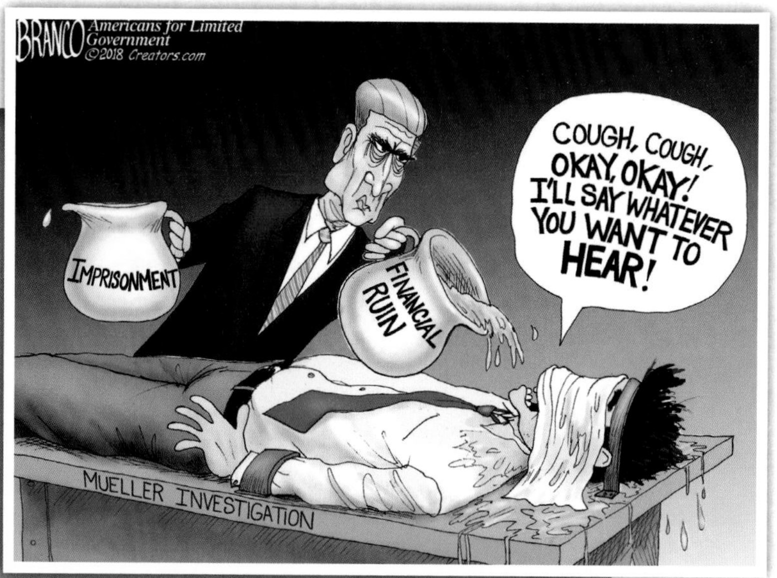
BRANCO Americans for Limited Government ©2018 Creators.com
COUGH, COUGH, OKAY, OKAY! I'LL SAY WHATEVER YOU WANT TO HEAR!
IMPRISONMENT
FINANCIAL RUIN
MUELLER INVESTIGATION

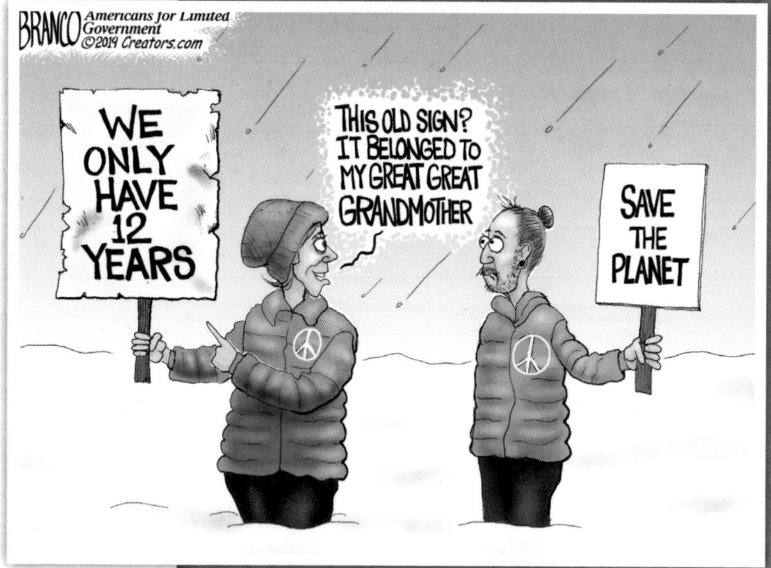
BRANCO Americans for Limited Government ©2019 Creators.com
WE ONLY HAVE 12 YEARS
THIS OLD SIGN? IT BELONGED TO MY GREAT GREAT GRANDMOTHER
SAVE THE PLANET

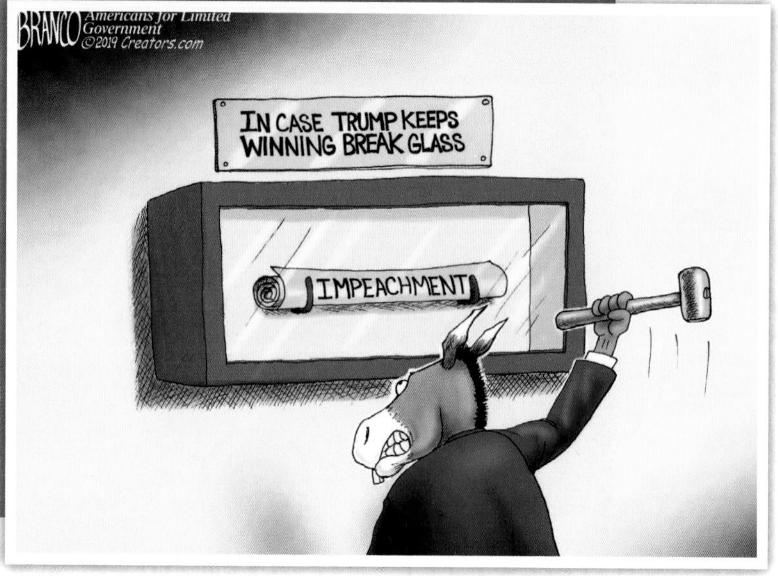
BRANCO Americans for Limited Government ©2019 Creators.com
IN CASE TRUMP KEEPS WINNING BREAK GLASS
IMPEACHMENT

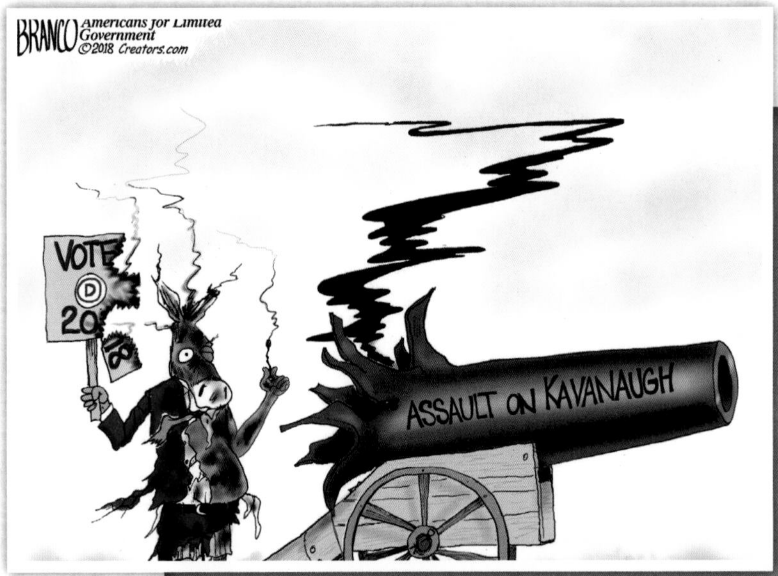
BRANCO Americans for Limited Government ©2018 Creators.com
VOTE
2018
ASSAULT ON KAVANAUGH

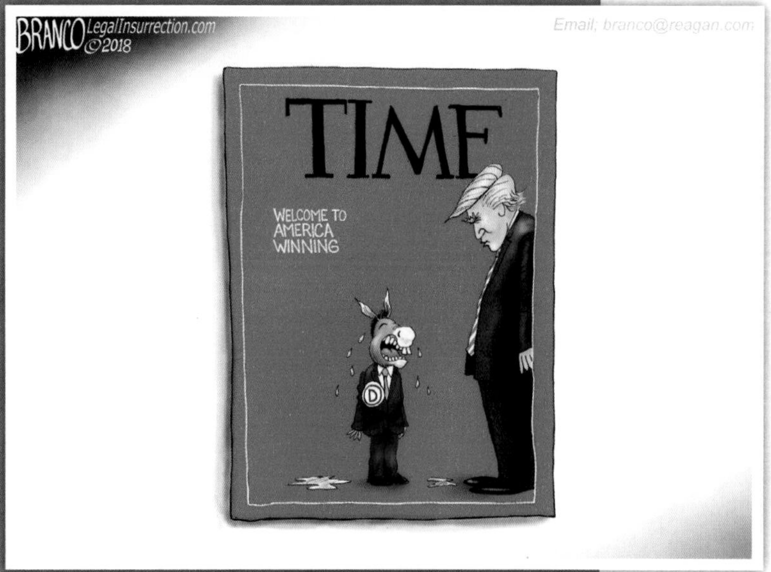
BRANCO LegalInsurrection.com ©2018
Email; branco@reagan.com
TIME
WELCOME TO AMERICA WINNING

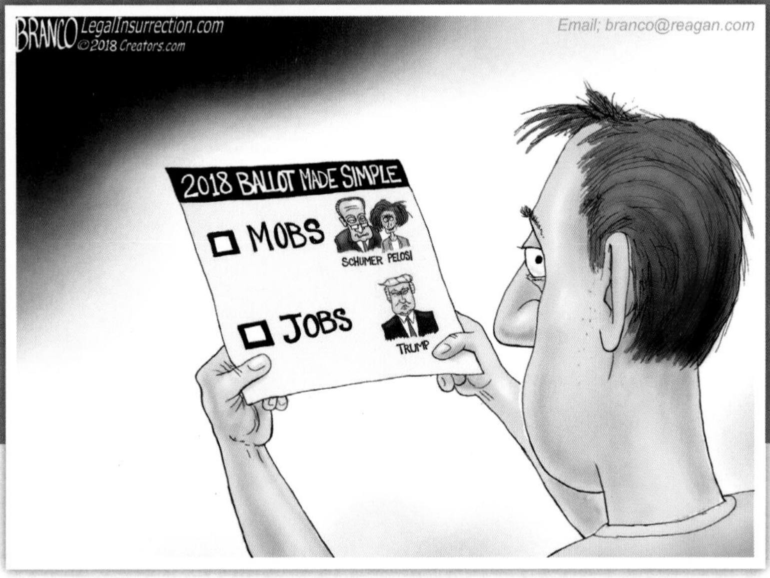
BRANCO LegalInsurrection.com ©2018 Creators.com
Email; branco@reagan.com
2018 BALLOT MADE SIMPLE
MOBS
SCHUMER PELOSI
JOBS
TRUMP

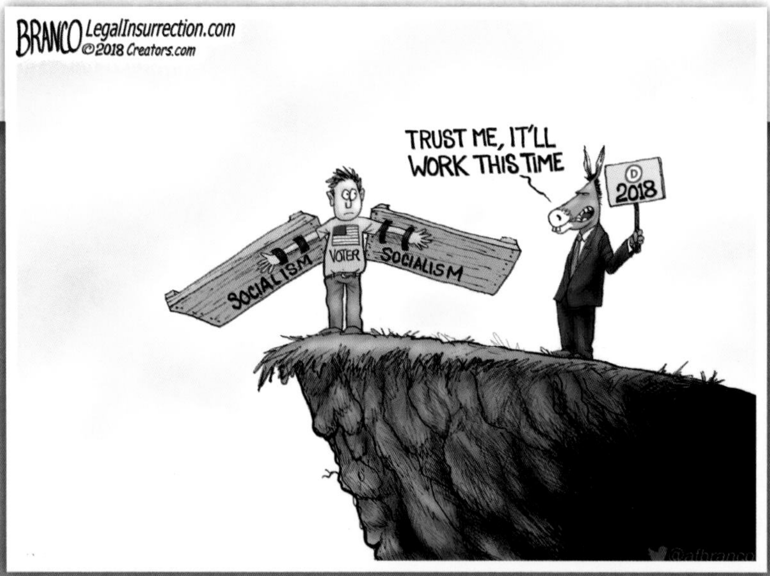
BRANCO LegalInsurrection.com
©2018 Creators.com
TRUST ME, IT'LL WORK THIS TIME
D
2018
SOCIALISM
VOTER
SOCIALISM

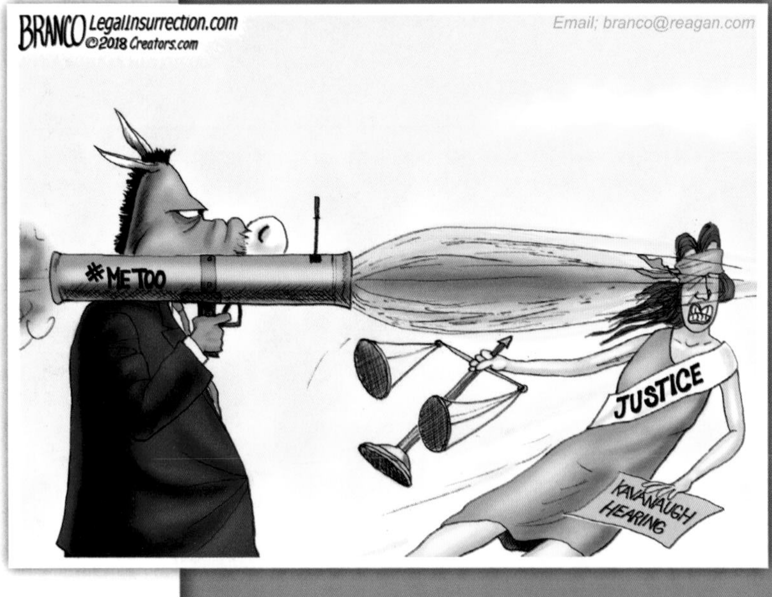
BRANCO LegalInsurrection.com
©2018 Creators.com
Email; branco@reagan.com
#METOO
JUSTICE
KAVANAUGH HEARING

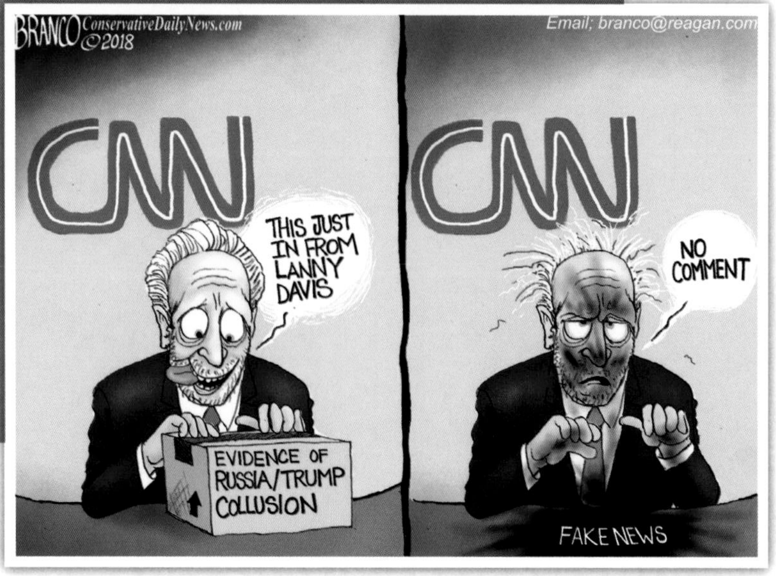
BRANCO ConservativeDailyNews.com
©2018
Email; branco@reagan.com
CNN
THIS JUST IN FROM LANNY DAVIS
EVIDENCE OF RUSSIA/TRUMP COLLUSION
CNN
NO COMMENT
FAKE NEWS

BRANCO LegalInsurrection.com ©2018
TRUMP IS STIFLING MY FREE SPEECH!
SECURITY CLEARANCE REVOKED
BRENNAN
Email: branco@reagan.com

BRANCO ConservativeDailyNews.com ©2018
Email; branco@reagan.com
A PHOTO WORTH A 1000 WORDS
SEE! TRUMP IS HITLER!
MSMEDIA
2014 PHOTO

BRANCO ConservativeDailyNews.com ©2018
Email; branco@reagan.com
AMERICA WAS NEVER GREAT!
ANDREW CUOMO FOR PRESIDENT 2020
GOV CUOMO
TRASH TALK

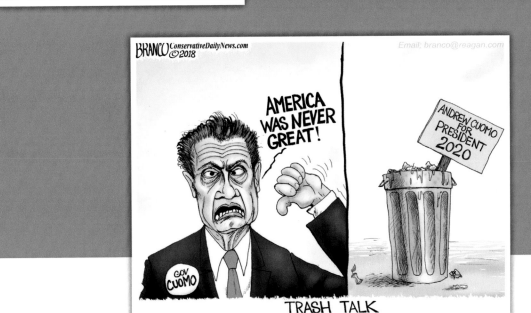

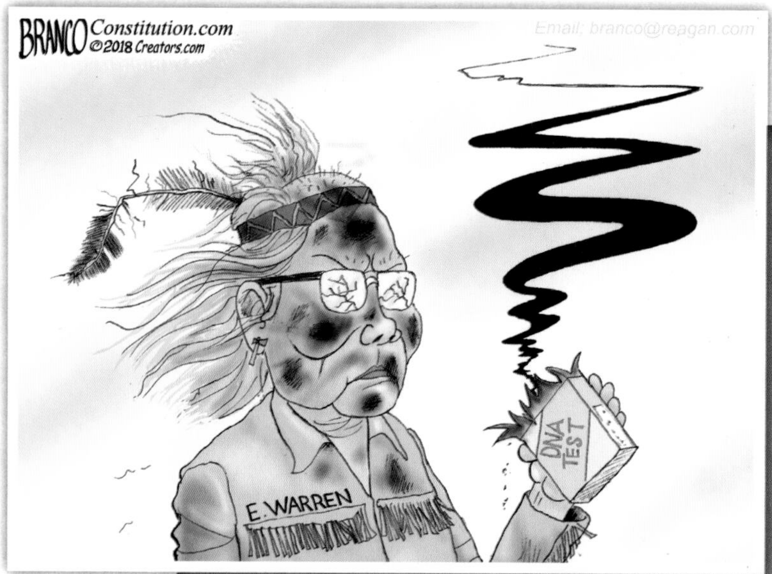
BRANCO Constitution.com
©2018 Creators.com
Email: branco@reagan.com
E.WARREN
DNA TEST

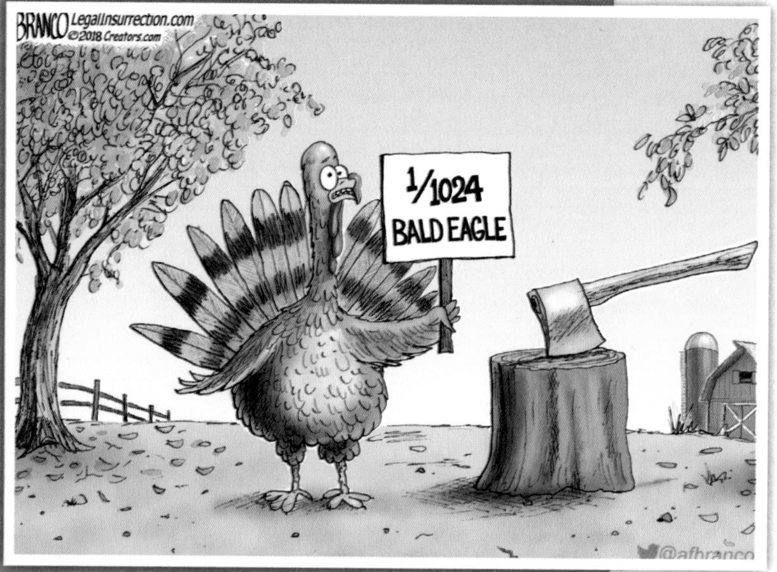
BRANCO LegalInsurrection.com
©2018 Creators.com
1/1024
BALD EAGLE
@afbranco

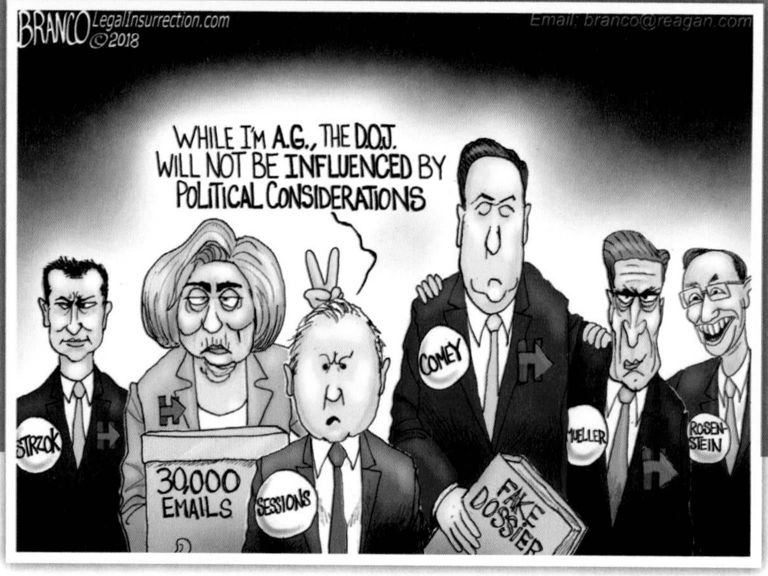
BRANCO LegalInsurrection.com
©2018
Email: branco@reagan.com
WHILE I'M A.G., THE D.O.J. WILL NOT BE INFLUENCED BY POLITICAL CONSIDERATIONS
STRZOK
30,000 EMAILS
SESSIONS
COMEY
FAKE DOSSIER
MUELLER
ROSEN-STEIN

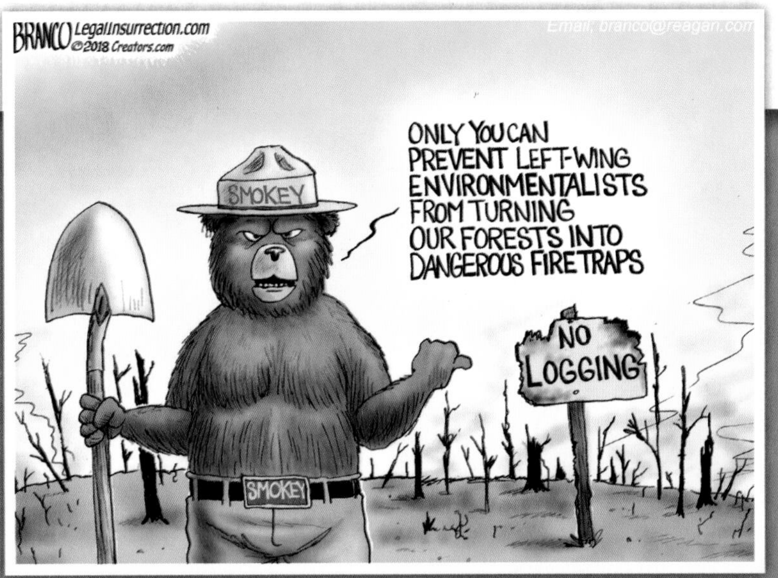
BRANCO LegalInsurrection.com
©2018 Creators.com
Email; branco@reagan.com
SMOKEY
ONLY YOU CAN PREVENT LEFT-WING ENVIRONMENTALISTS FROM TURNING OUR FORESTS INTO DANGEROUS FIRETRAPS
NO LOGGING
SMOKEY

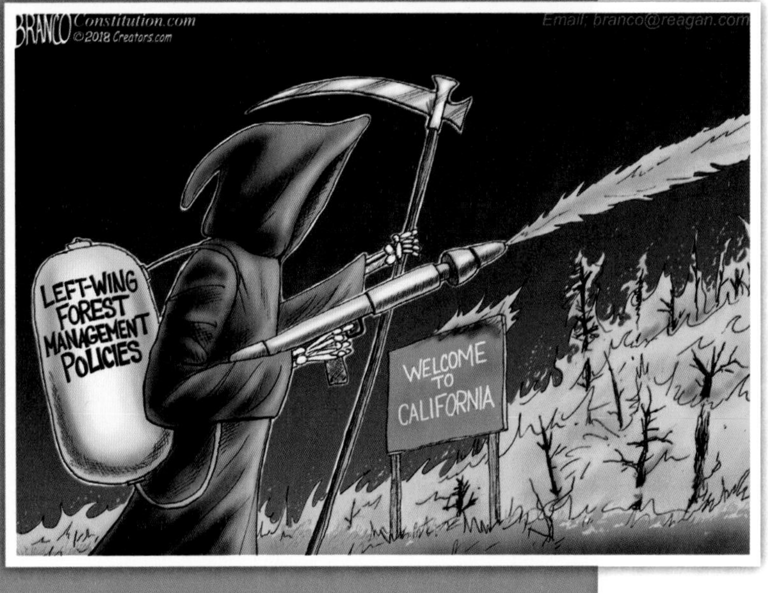
BRANCO Constitution.com
©2018 Creators.com
Email; branco@reagan.com
LEFT-WING FOREST MANAGEMENT POLICIES
WELCOME TO CALIFORNIA

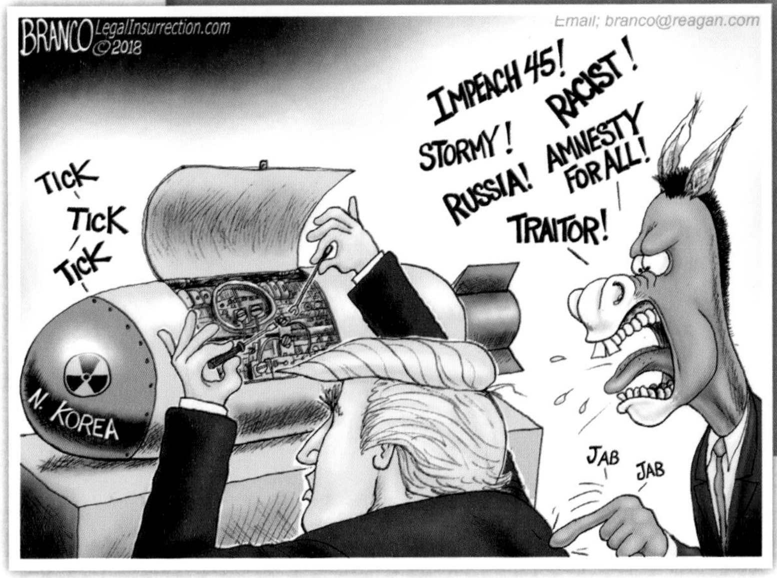
BRANCO LegalInsurrection.com
©2018
Email; branco@reagan.com
TICK
TICK
TICK
IMPEACH 45!
RACIST!
STORMY!
AMNESTY FOR ALL!
RUSSIA!
TRAITOR!
N. KOREA
JAB
JAB

BRANCO ConservativeDailyNews.com ©2018
Email: branco@reagan.com
FREE AT LAST! FREE AT LAST!
THANK GOD ALMIGHTY, FREE AT LAST!
KANYE
LIBERALISM
CANDACE OWENS

BRANCO Americans for Limited Government ©2018 Creators.com
RECORD COLD AND SNOW GRIPS THE SOUTHEAST
MAKE GLOBAL WARMING GREAT AGAIN
AL GORE

BRANCO LegalInsurrection.com ©2018 Creators.com
The GRINCHES
ATTEMPTING TO STEAL THE PRESIDENCY
COMEY
MUELLER
SCHIFF
MSMEDIA

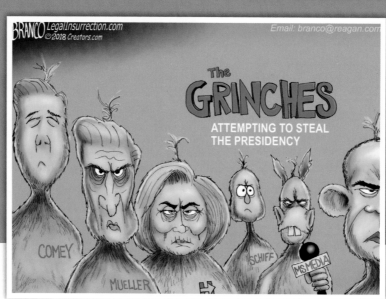

BRANCO Americans for Limited Government ©2018
THAT'S A STUPID HAT
AMERICA FIRST

BRANCO Americans for Limited Government ©2018 Creators.com
WHATA YA THINK?
Hillary 2020
LOCK HER UP! LOCK HER UP! LOCK HER UP! LOCK HER UP!

BRANCO Americans for Limited Government ©2018 Creators.com
THIS IS MY STORY AND I'M STICKING TO IT
CHRISTINE BLASEY FORD

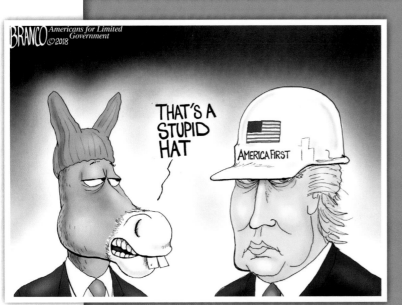

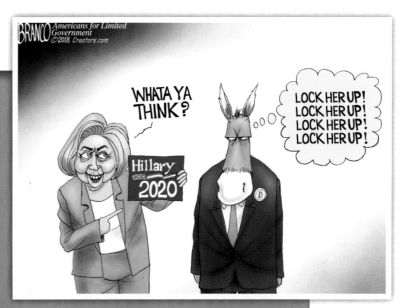

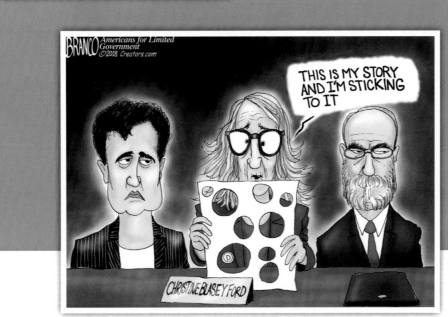

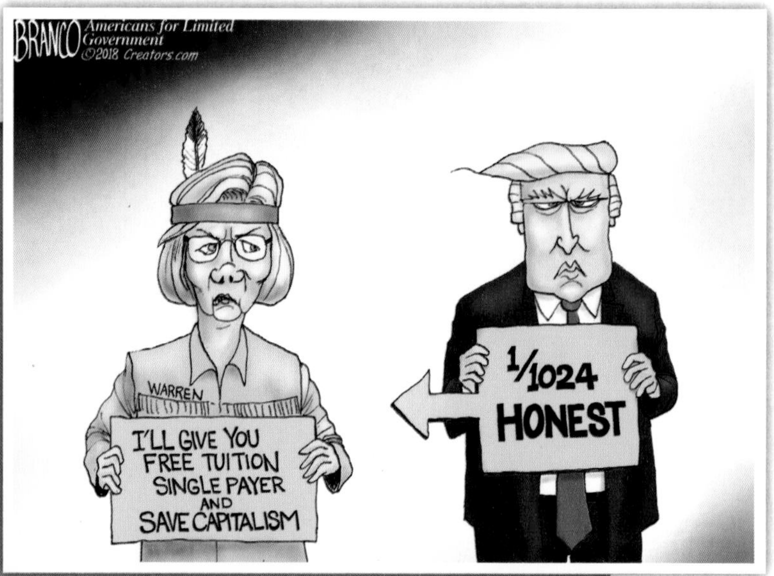
BRANCO Americans for Limited Government
©2018 Creators.com
WARREN
I'LL GIVE YOU FREE TUITION SINGLE PAYER AND SAVE CAPITALISM
1/1024 HONEST

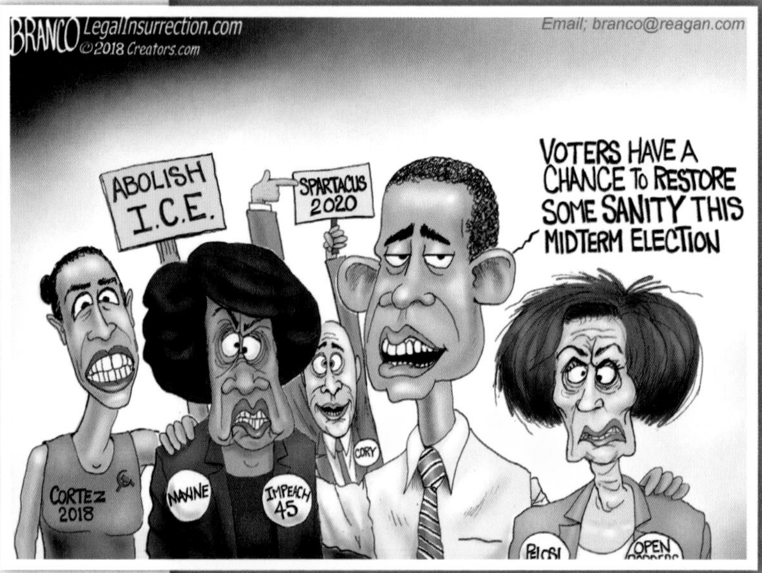
BRANCO LegalInsurrection.com
©2018 Creators.com
Email; branco@reagan.com
ABOLISH I.C.E.
SPARTACUS 2020
VOTERS HAVE A CHANCE TO RESTORE SOME SANITY THIS MIDTERM ELECTION
CORTEZ 2018
MAXINE
IMPEACH 45
CORY
PELOSI
OPEN

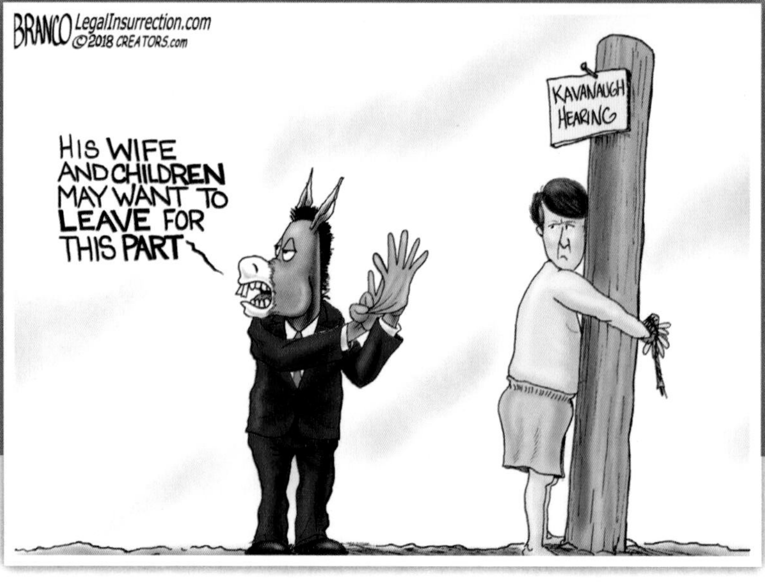
BRANCO LegalInsurrection.com
©2018 CREATORS.com
KAVANAUGH HEARING
HIS WIFE AND CHILDREN MAY WANT TO LEAVE FOR THIS PART

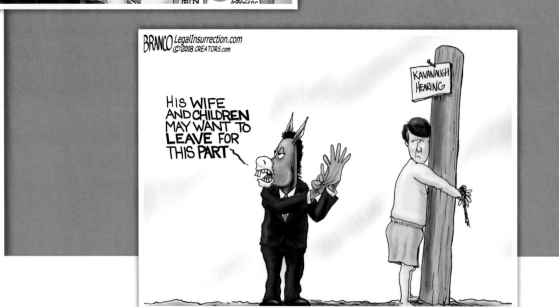

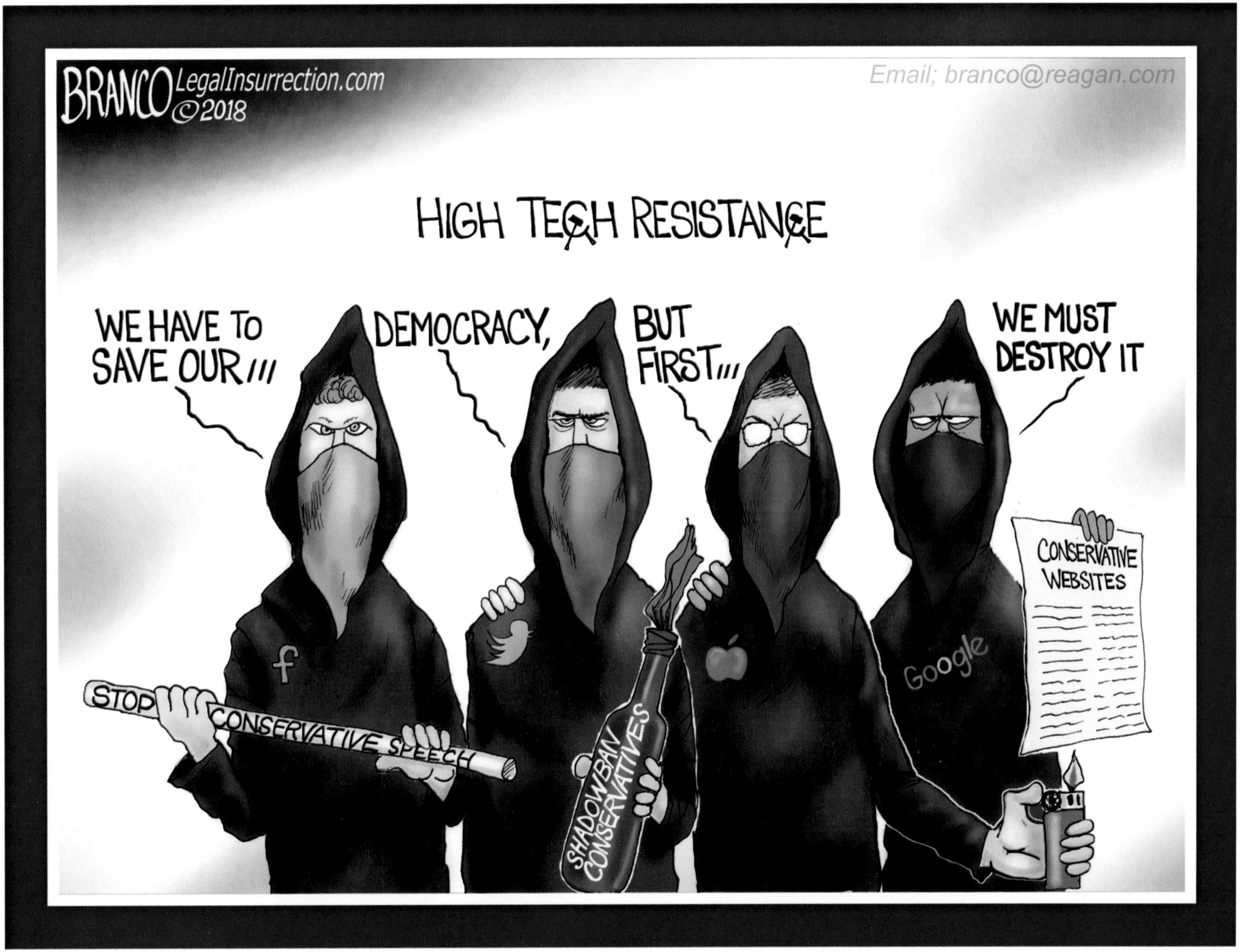
BRANCO LegalInsurrection.com ©2018
Email; branco@reagan.com
HIGH TECH RESISTANCE
WE HAVE TO SAVE OUR,,,
DEMOCRACY,
BUT FIRST,,,
WE MUST DESTROY IT
STOP CONSERVATIVE SPEECH
SHADOWBAN CONSERVATIVES
CONSERVATIVE WEBSITES
Google

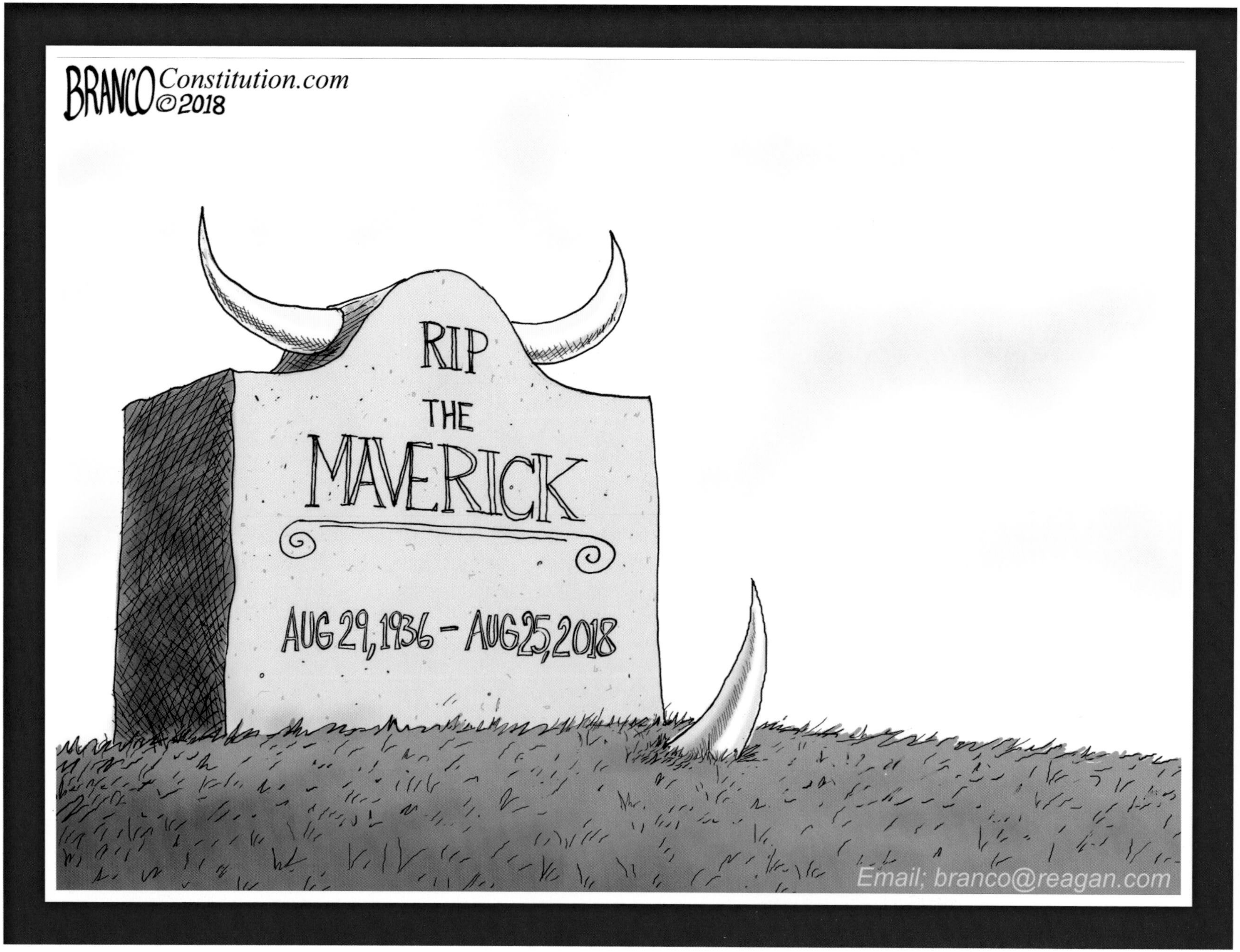
BRANCO Constitution.com
©2018
RIP
THE
MAVERICK
AUG 29, 1936 - AUG 25, 2018
Email; branco@reagan.com

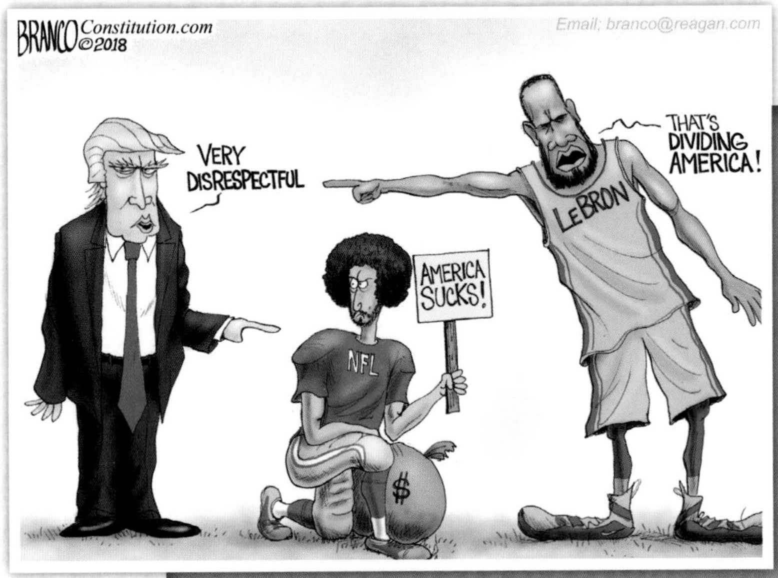
BRANCO Constitution.com ©2018
Email; branco@reagan.com
VERY DISRESPECTFUL
AMERICA SUCKS!
NFL
$
THAT'S DIVIDING AMERICA!
LeBRON

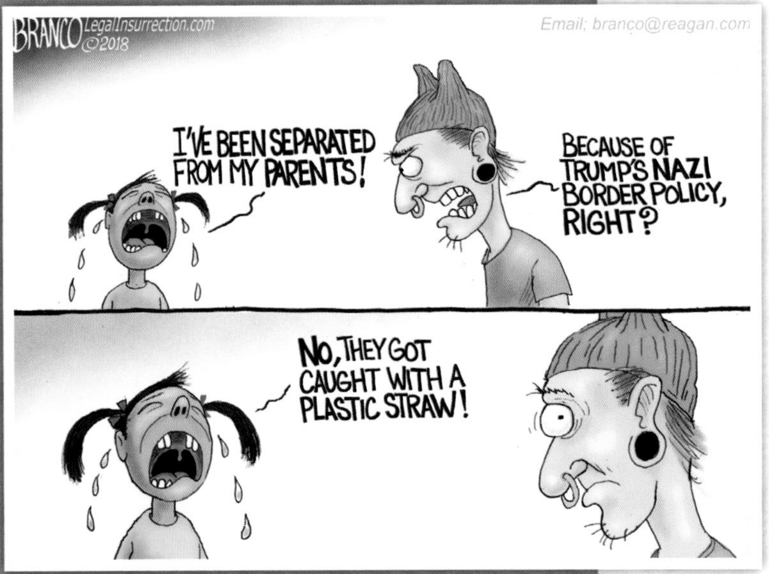
BRANCO LegalInsurrection.com ©2018
Email; branco@reagan.com
I'VE BEEN SEPARATED FROM MY PARENTS!
BECAUSE OF TRUMP'S NAZI BORDER POLICY, RIGHT?
NO, THEY GOT CAUGHT WITH A PLASTIC STRAW!

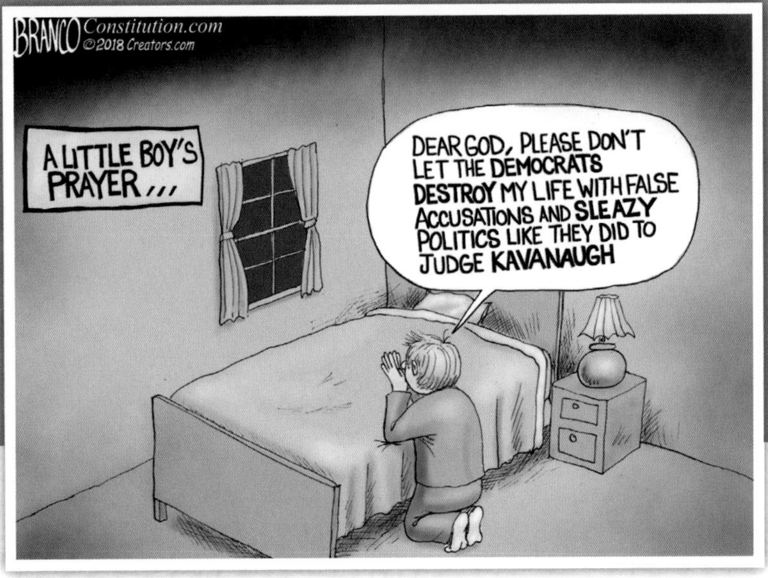
BRANCO Constitution.com ©2018 Creators.com
A LITTLE BOY'S PRAYER...
DEAR GOD, PLEASE DON'T LET THE DEMOCRATS DESTROY MY LIFE WITH FALSE ACCUSATIONS AND SLEAZY POLITICS LIKE THEY DID TO JUDGE KAVANAUGH

BRANCO LegalInsurrection.com ©2018 CREATORS.com
Email; branco@reagan.com
IRAN
RUSSIANS!
AMERICAN ELECTION SYSTEM
CHINA

BRANCO Americans for Limited Government ©2018 Creators.com
GLOBALISM
HOLLY-WOOD

BRANCO Americans for Limited Government ©2018
THE SWAMP
IG REPORT
THERE IS NO SWAMP

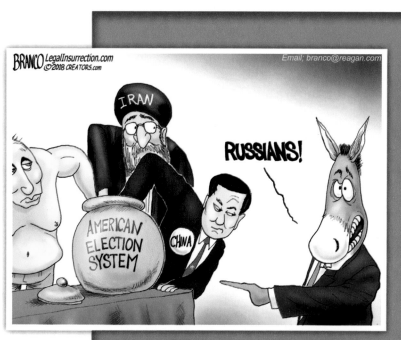

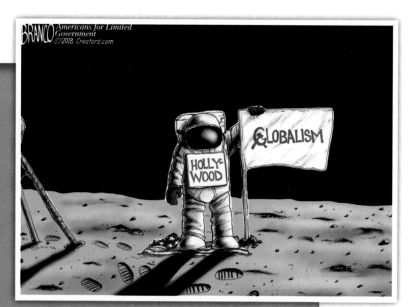

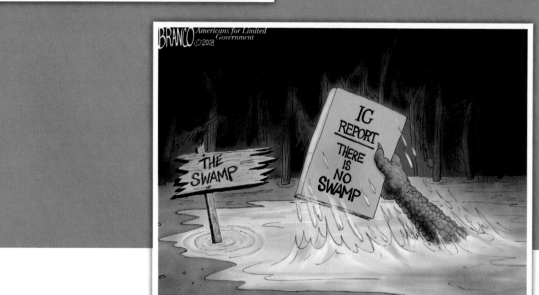

BRANCO Constitution.com
©2018 Creators.com
Email; branco@reagan.com
DOJ
I DON'T SMELL ANYTHING
HILLARY CRIMES AND CORRUPTION
DEEP STATE CORRUPTION
SESSIONS

BRANCO LegalInsurrection.com
©2018 CREATORS.com
Email; branco@reagan.com
I BUILT THAT!
OBAMA-NOMICS
US BUSINESSES 2009 2016
REGULATIONS
TAXES
BEST ECONOMY IN U.S. HISTORY
US BUSINESSES 2017 2018
DEREGULATION AND TAX CUTS

BRANCO Constitution.com
©2018
Email; branco@reagan.com
OBAMA LEGACY
IRAN DEAL
OPEN BORDERS
PARIS CLIMATE ACCORD
EXC. ORDERS

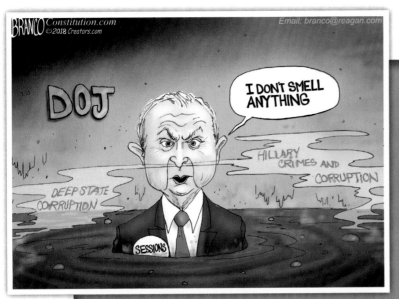

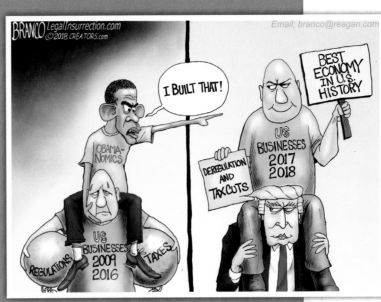

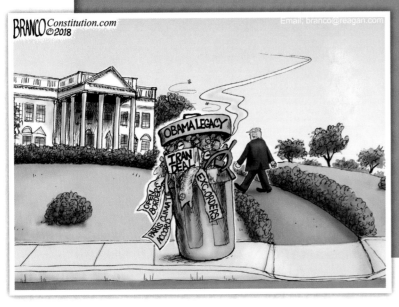

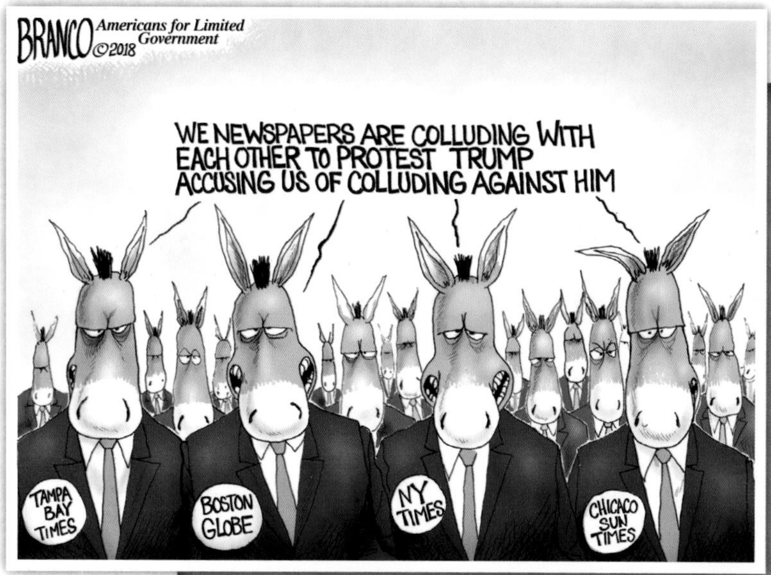
BRANCO ©2018 Americans for Limited Government
WE NEWSPAPERS ARE COLLUDING WITH EACH OTHER TO PROTEST TRUMP ACCUSING US OF COLLUDING AGAINST HIM
TAMPA BAY TIMES
BOSTON GLOBE
NY TIMES
CHICAGO SUN TIMES

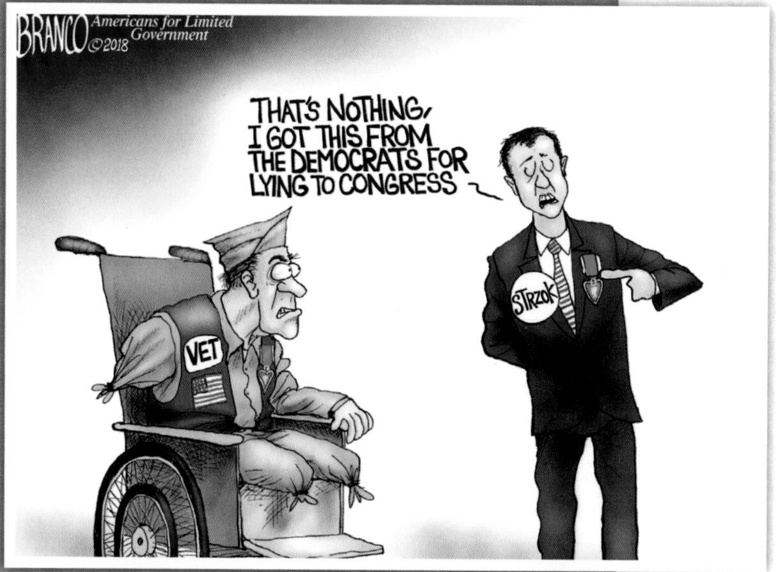
BRANCO ©2018 Americans for Limited Government
THAT'S NOTHING, I GOT THIS FROM THE DEMOCRATS FOR LYING TO CONGRESS
VET
STRZOK

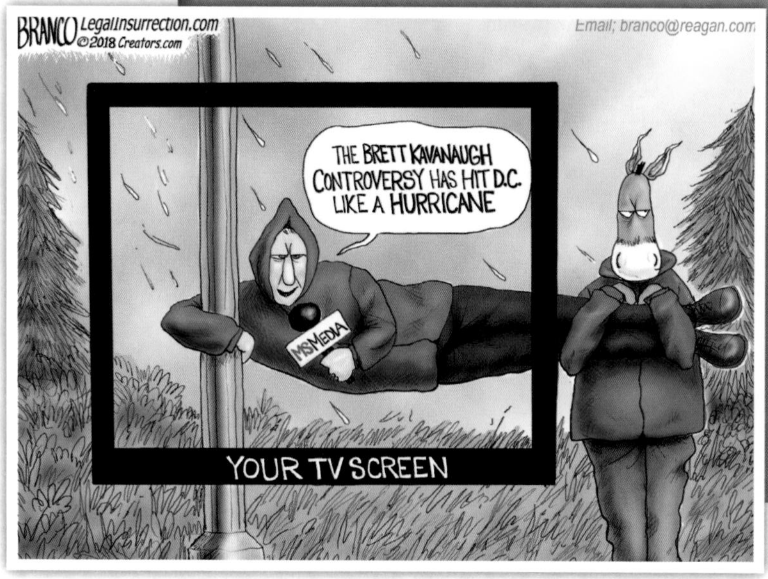
BRANCO LegalInsurrection.com ©2018 Creators.com
Email; branco@reagan.com
THE BRETT KAVANAUGH CONTROVERSY HAS HIT D.C. LIKE A HURRICANE
MSMEDIA
YOUR TV SCREEN

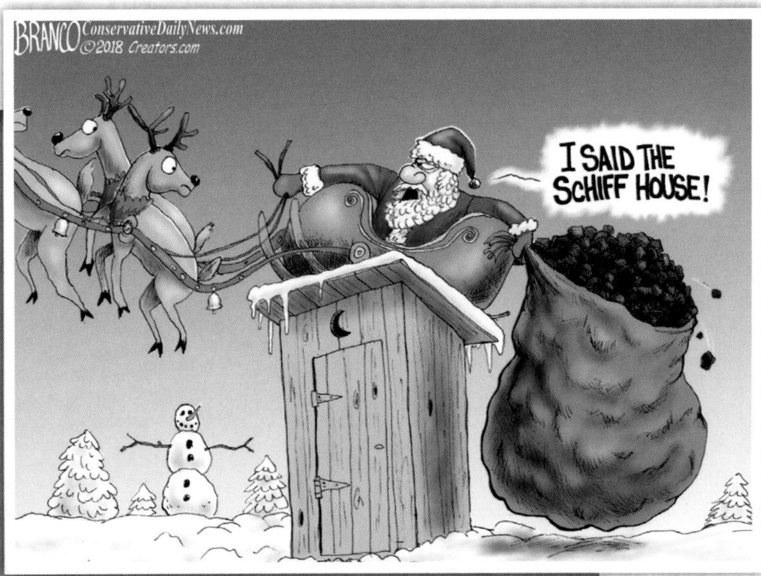
BRANCO ConservativeDailyNews.com ©2018 Creators.com
I SAID THE SCHIFF HOUSE!

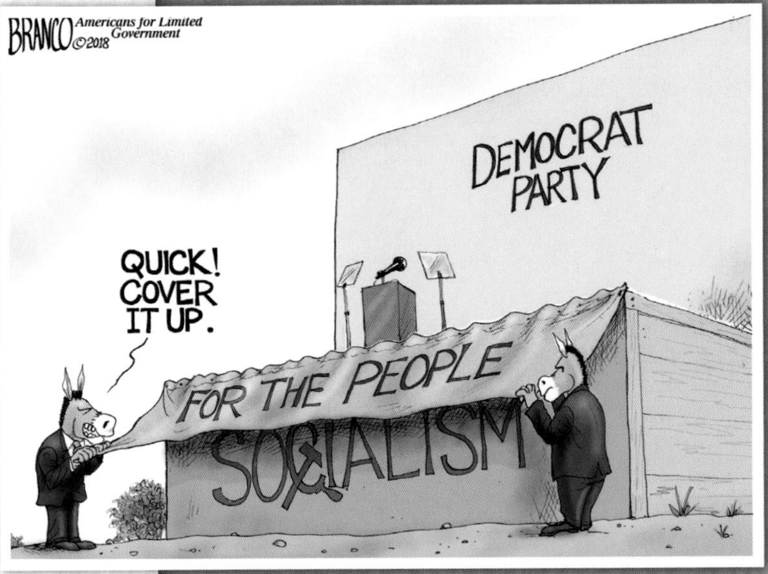
BRANCO Americans for Limited Government ©2018
DEMOCRAT PARTY
QUICK! COVER IT UP.
FOR THE PEOPLE
SOCIALISM

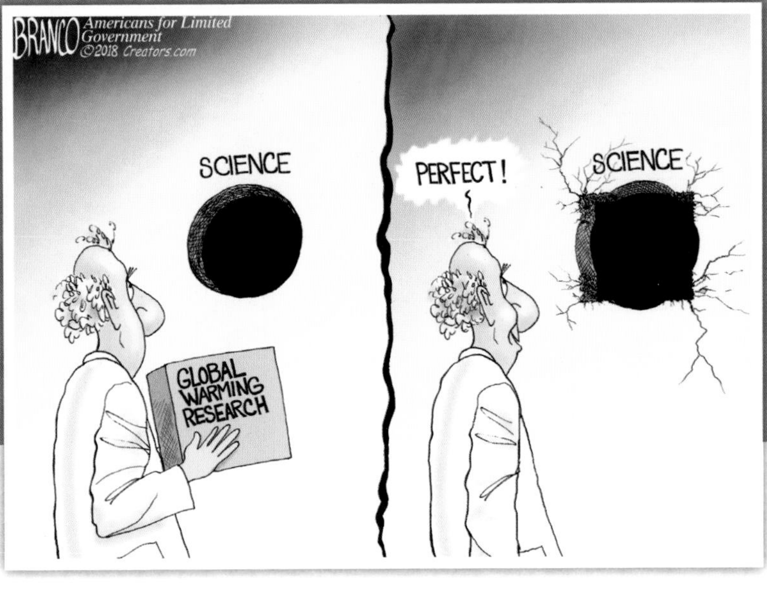
BRANCO Americans for Limited Government ©2018 Creators.com
SCIENCE
GLOBAL WARMING RESEARCH
PERFECT!
SCIENCE

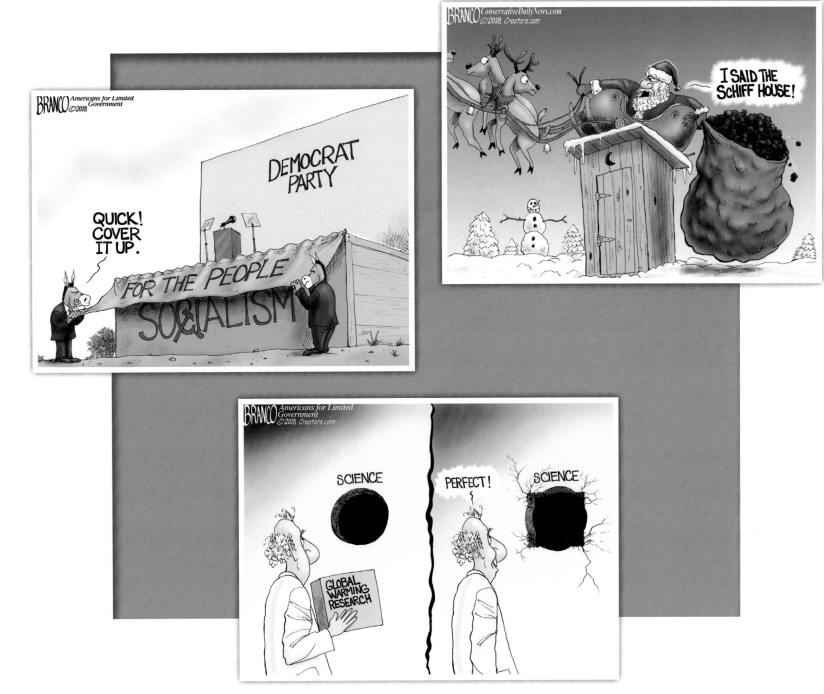

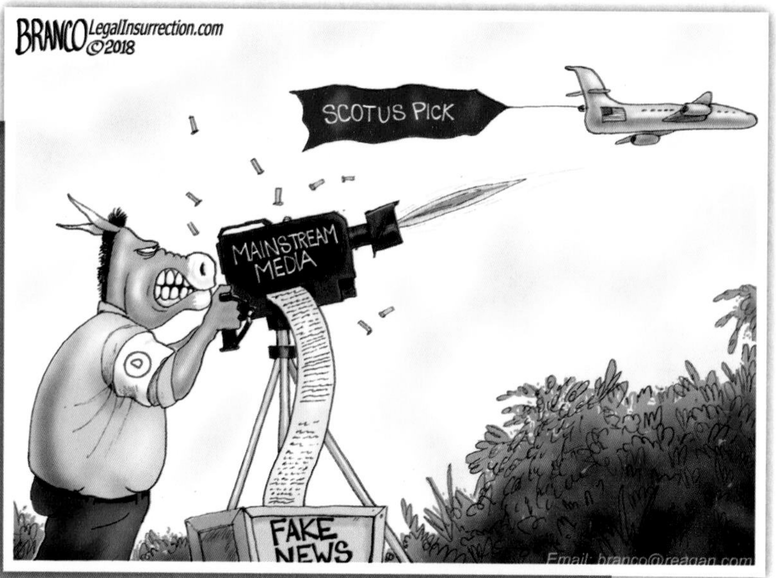
BRANCO LegalInsurrection.com ©2018
SCOTUS PICK
MAINSTREAM MEDIA
FAKE NEWS
Email: branco@reagan.com

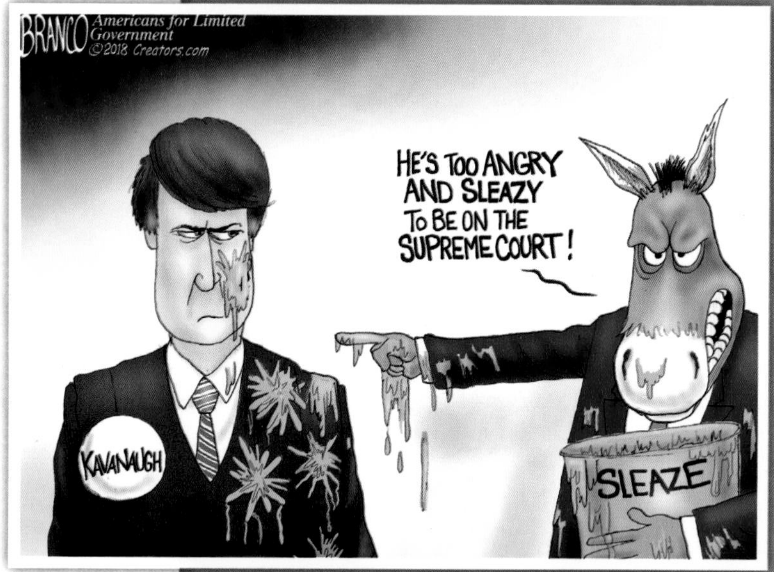
BRANCO Americans for Limited Government ©2018 Creators.com
HE'S TOO ANGRY AND SLEAZY TO BE ON THE SUPREME COURT!
KAVANAUGH
SLEAZE

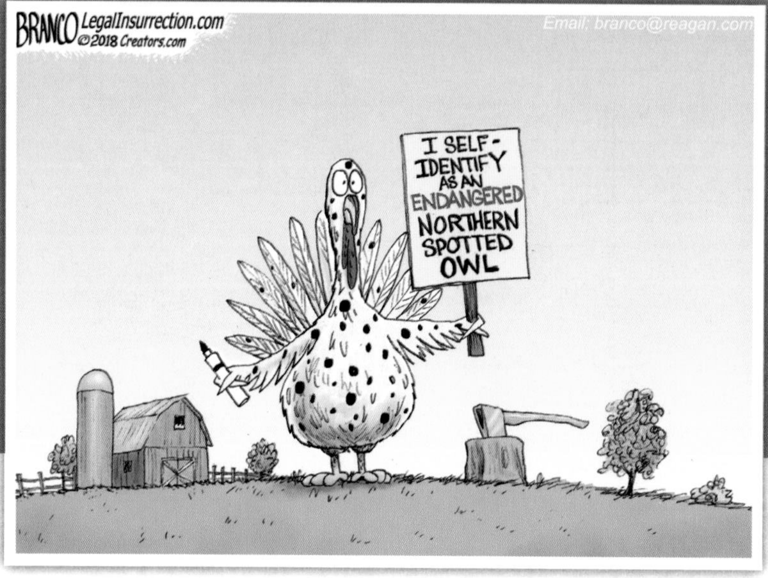
BRANCO LegalInsurrection.com ©2018 Creators.com
Email: branco@reagan.com
I SELF-IDENTIFY AS AN ENDANGERED NORTHERN SPOTTED OWL

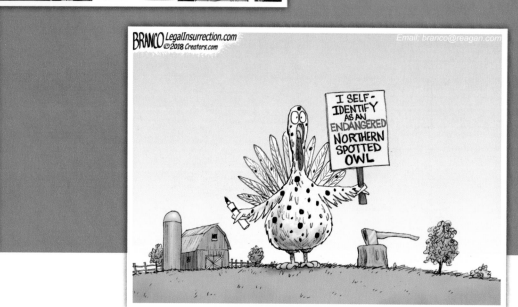

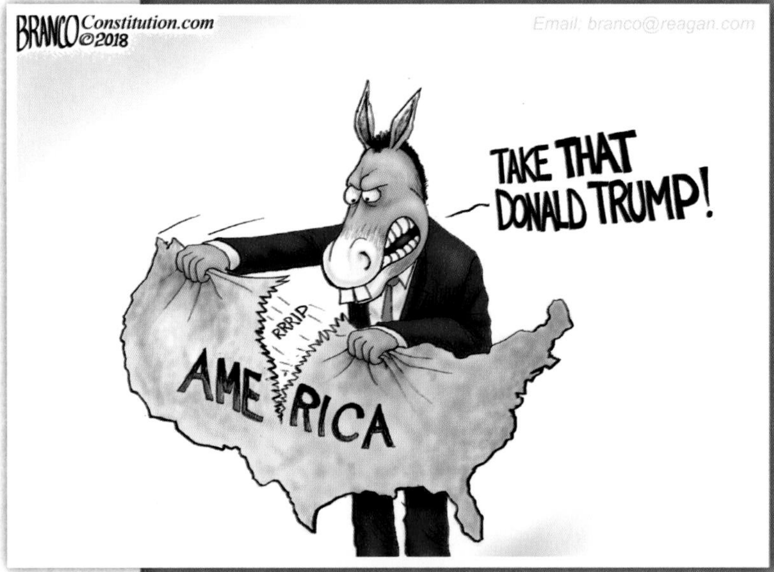
BRANCO Constitution.com ©2018
Email; branco@reagan.com
TAKE THAT DONALD TRUMP!
RRRIP
AMERICA

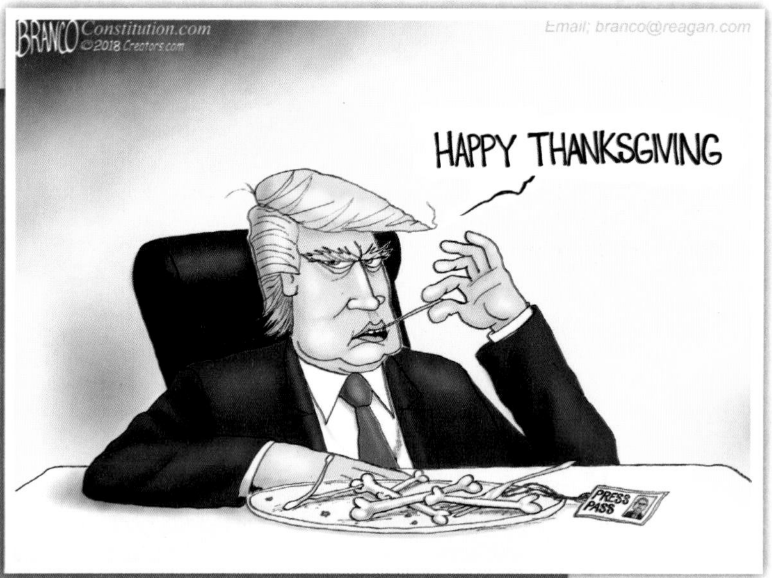
BRANCO Constitution.com ©2018 Creators.com
Email; branco@reagan.com
HAPPY THANKSGIVING
PRESS PASS

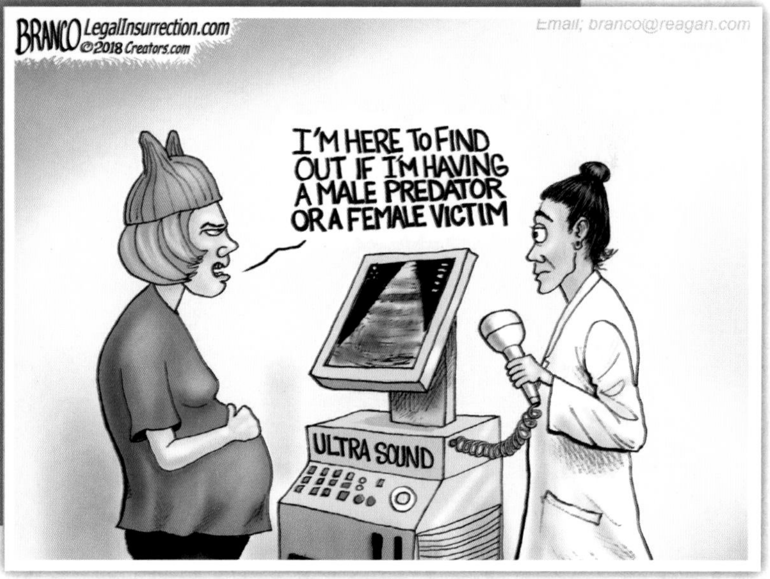
BRANCO LegalInsurrection.com ©2018 Creators.com
Email; branco@reagan.com
I'M HERE TO FIND OUT IF I'M HAVING A MALE PREDATOR OR A FEMALE VICTIM
ULTRA SOUND

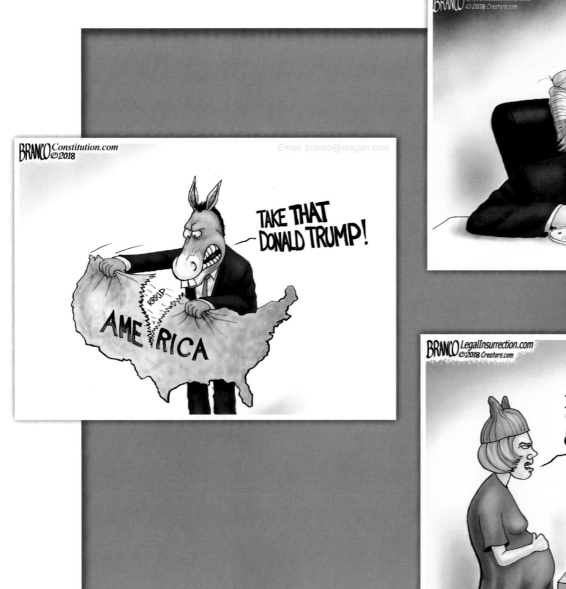

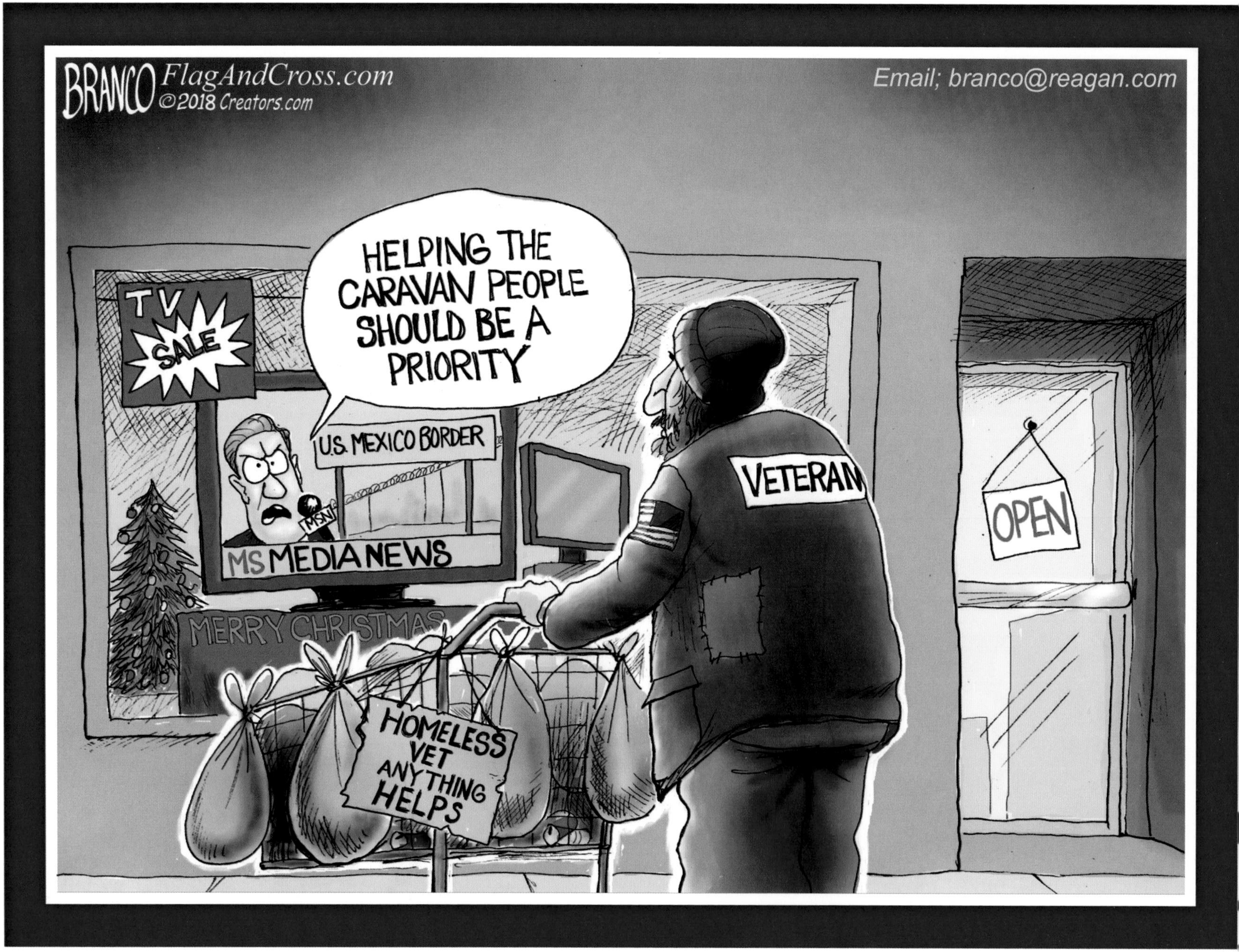
BRANCO FlagAndCross.com
©2018 Creators.com
Email; branco@reagan.com
HELPING THE CARAVAN PEOPLE SHOULD BE A PRIORITY
TV SALE
U.S. MEXICO BORDER
MSN
MS MEDIA NEWS
MERRY CHRISTMAS
VETERAN
OPEN
HOMELESS VET ANYTHING HELPS

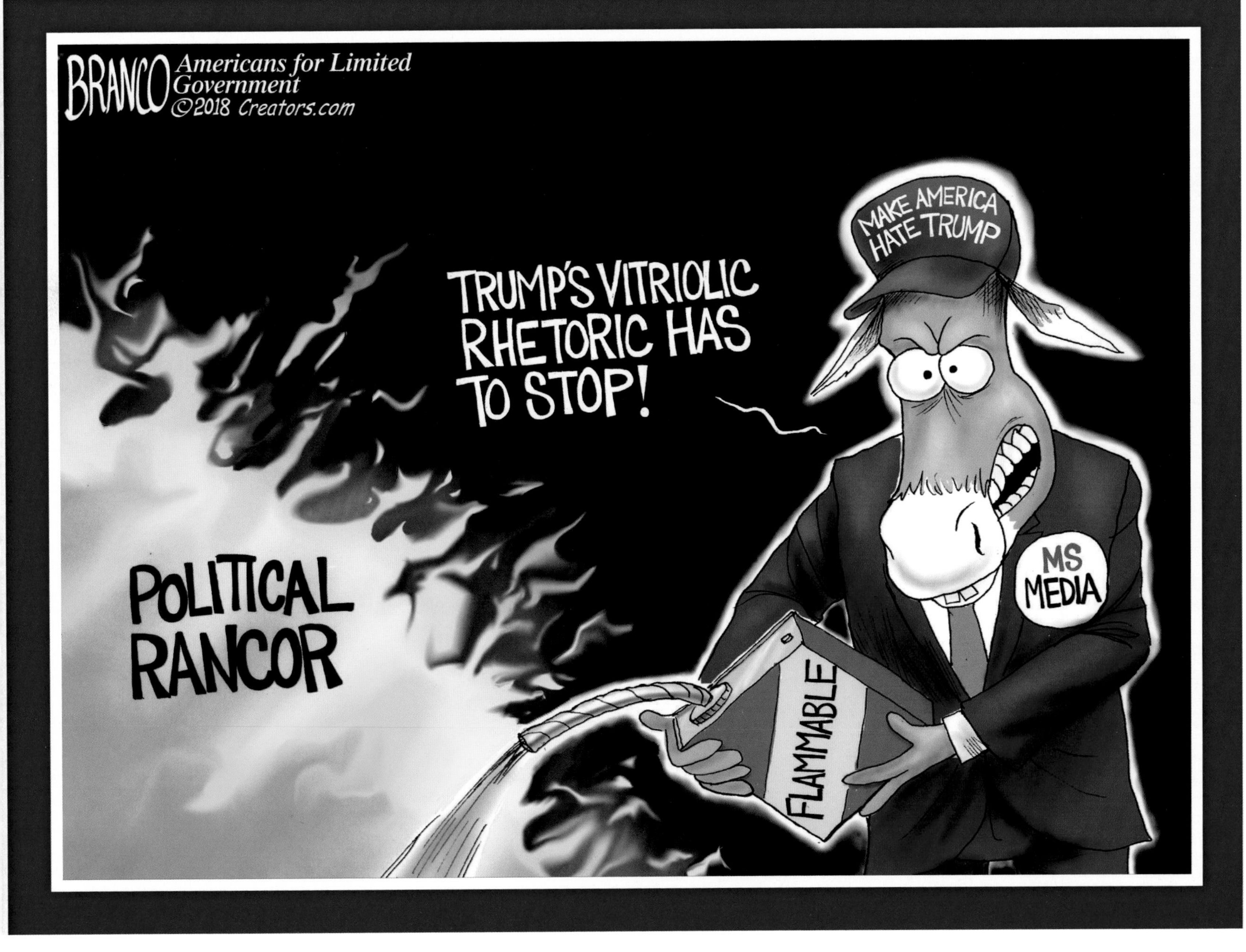
BRANCO Americans for Limited Government ©2018 Creators.com
MAKE AMERICA HATE TRUMP
TRUMP'S VITRIOLIC RHETORIC HAS TO STOP!
POLITICAL RANCOR
MS MEDIA
FLAMMABLE

Keeping America Great

BRANCO Americans for Limited Government ©2020 Creators.com
OBAMA RED LINE
TRUMP RED LINE

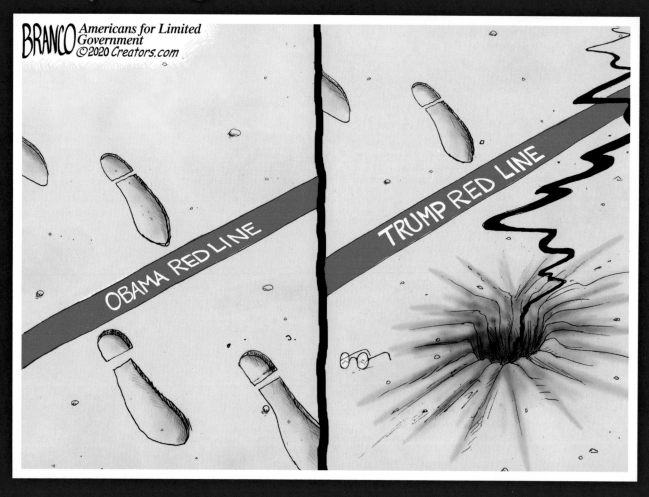

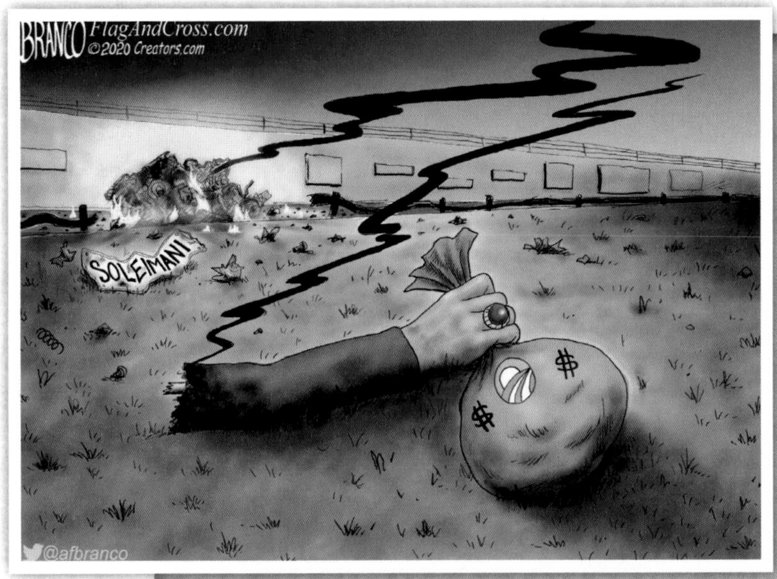
BRANCO FlagAndCross.com
©2020 Creators.com
SOLEIMANI
@afbranco

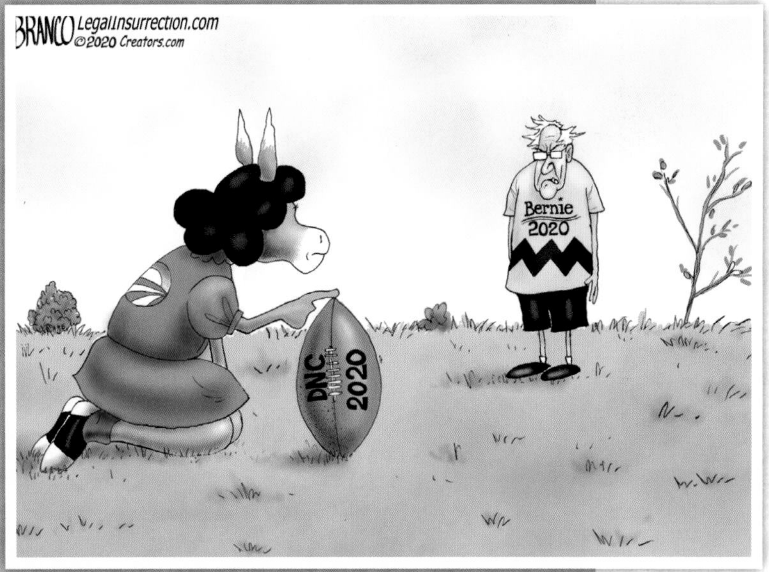
BRANCO LegalInsurrection.com
©2020 Creators.com
Bernie
2020
DNC
2020

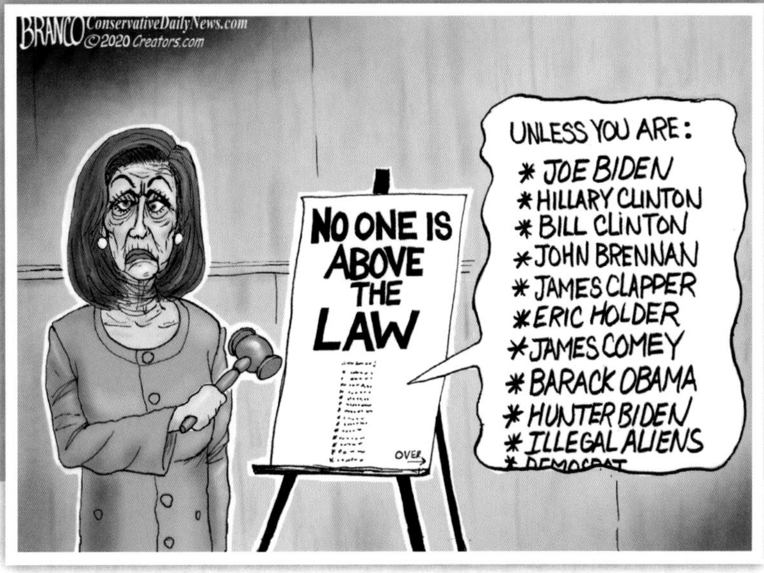
BRANCO ConservativeDailyNews.com
©2020 Creators.com
NO ONE IS ABOVE THE LAW
OVER
UNLESS YOU ARE:
* JOE BIDEN
* HILLARY CLINTON
* BILL CLINTON
* JOHN BRENNAN
* JAMES CLAPPER
* ERIC HOLDER
* JAMES COMEY
* BARACK OBAMA
* HUNTER BIDEN
* ILLEGAL ALIENS

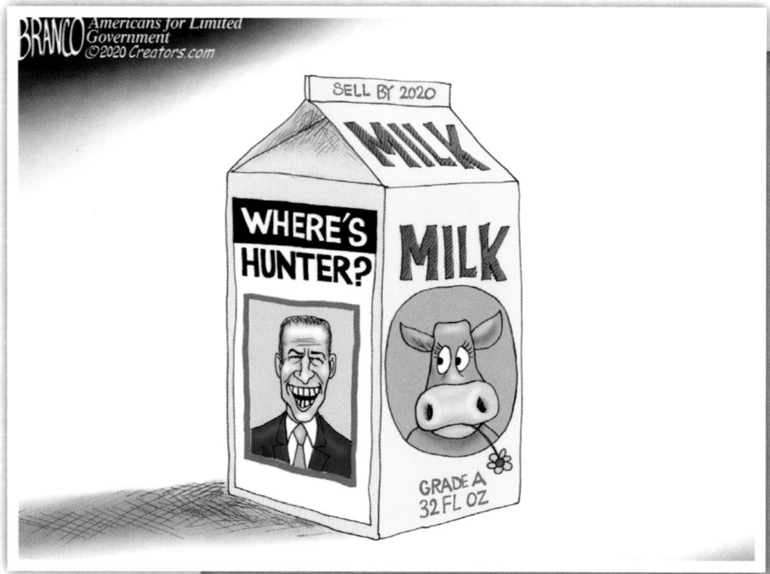
BRANCO Americans for Limited Government ©2020 Creators.com
SELL BY 2020
MILK
WHERE'S HUNTER?
MILK
GRADE A
32 FL OZ

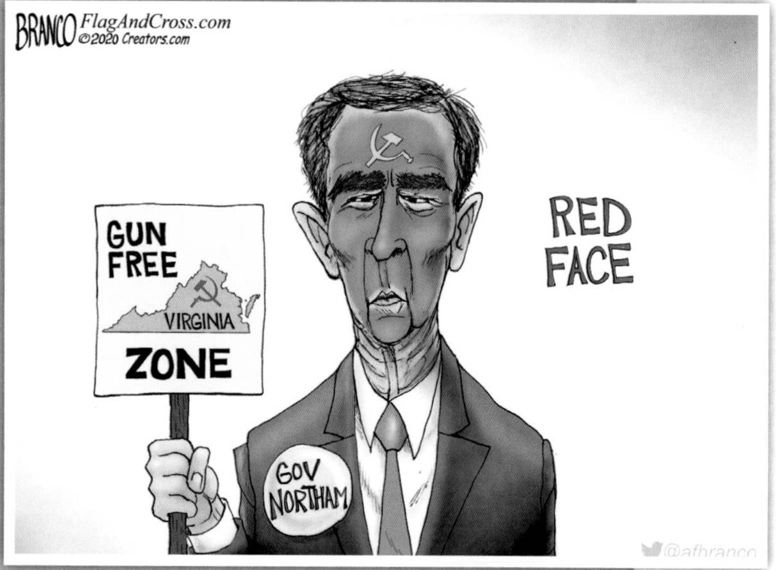
BRANCO FlagAndCross.com ©2020 Creators.com
GUN FREE
VIRGINIA
ZONE
RED FACE
GOV NORTHAM
@afbranco

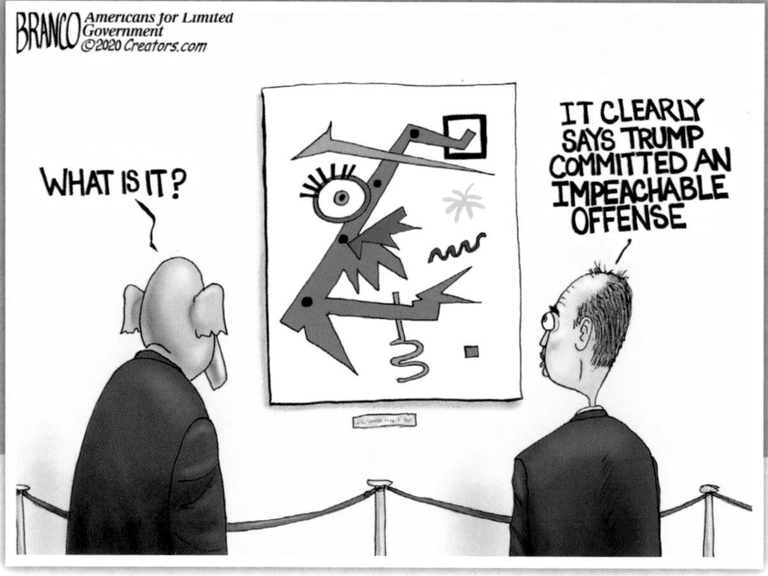
BRANCO Americans for Limited Government ©2020 Creators.com
WHAT IS IT?
IT CLEARLY SAYS TRUMP COMMITTED AN IMPEACHABLE OFFENSE

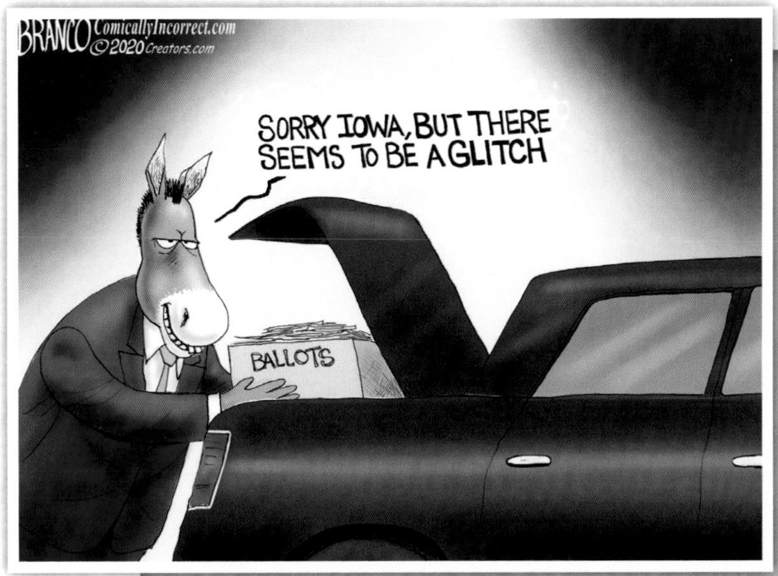
BRANCO ComicallyIncorrect.com ©2020 Creators.com
SORRY IOWA, BUT THERE SEEMS TO BE A GLITCH
BALLOTS

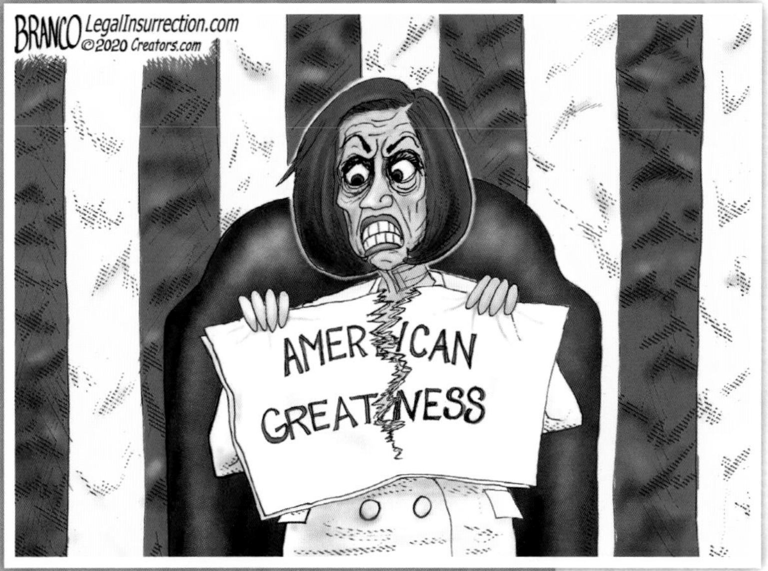
BRANCO LegalInsurrection.com ©2020 Creators.com
AMERICAN GREATNESS

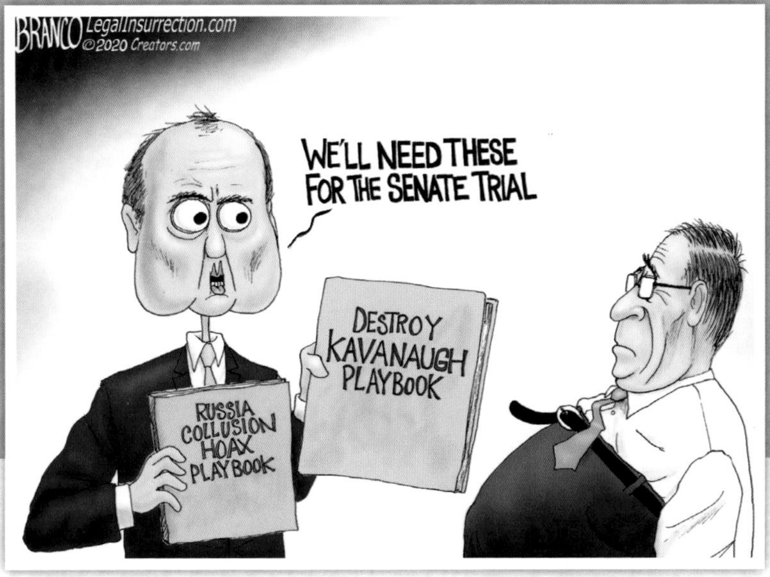
BRANCO LegalInsurrection.com ©2020 Creators.com
WE'LL NEED THESE FOR THE SENATE TRIAL
DESTROY KAVANAUGH PLAYBOOK
RUSSIA COLLUSION HOAX PLAYBOOK

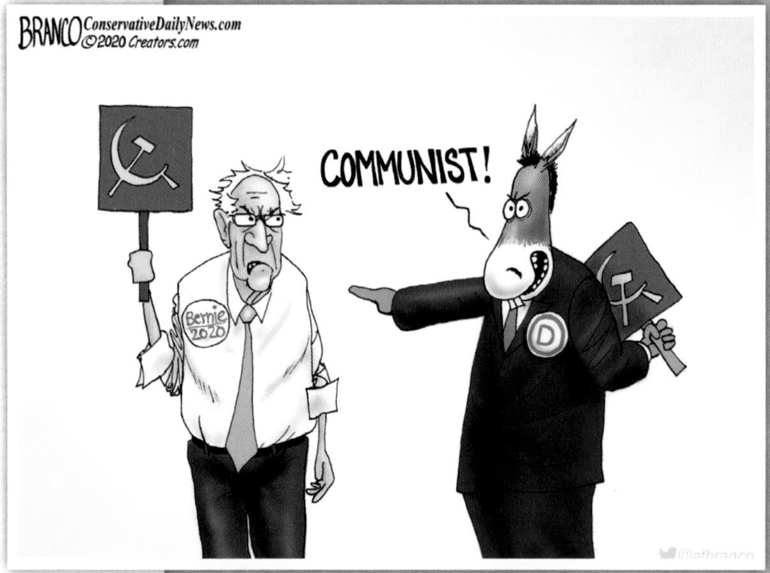
BRANCO ConservativeDailyNews.com ©2020 Creators.com
COMMUNIST!
Bernie 2020
D

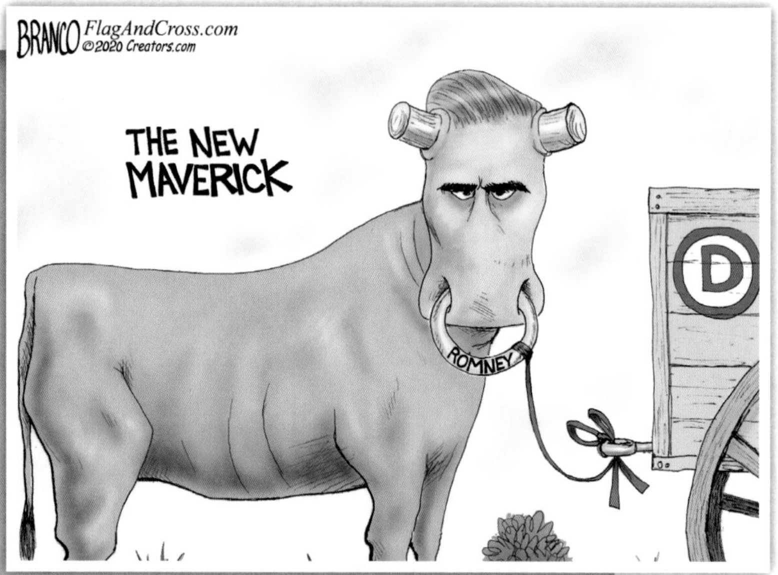
BRANCO FlagAndCross.com ©2020 Creators.com
THE NEW MAVERICK
ROMNEY
D

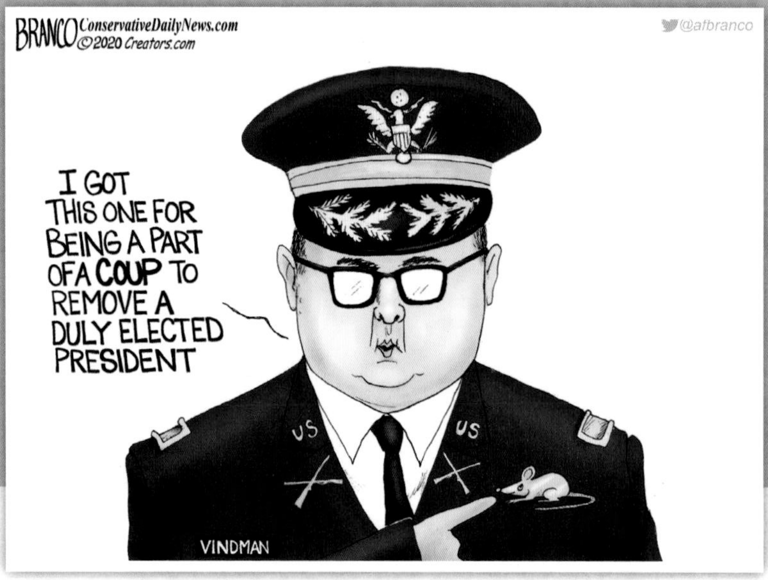
BRANCO ConservativeDailyNews.com ©2020 Creators.com
@afbranco
I GOT THIS ONE FOR BEING A PART OF A COUP TO REMOVE A DULY ELECTED PRESIDENT
US
US
VINDMAN

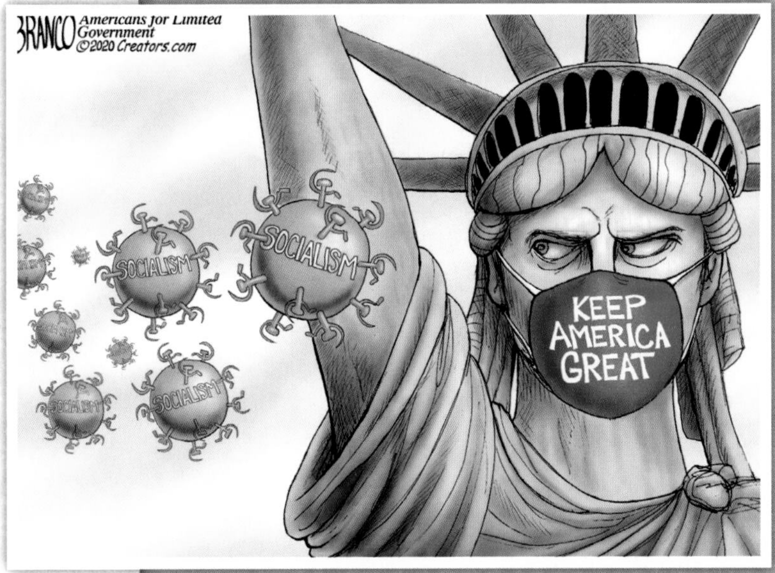
BRANCO Americans for Limited Government ©2020 Creators.com
SOCIALISM
SOCIALISM
SOCIALISM
KEEP AMERICA GREAT

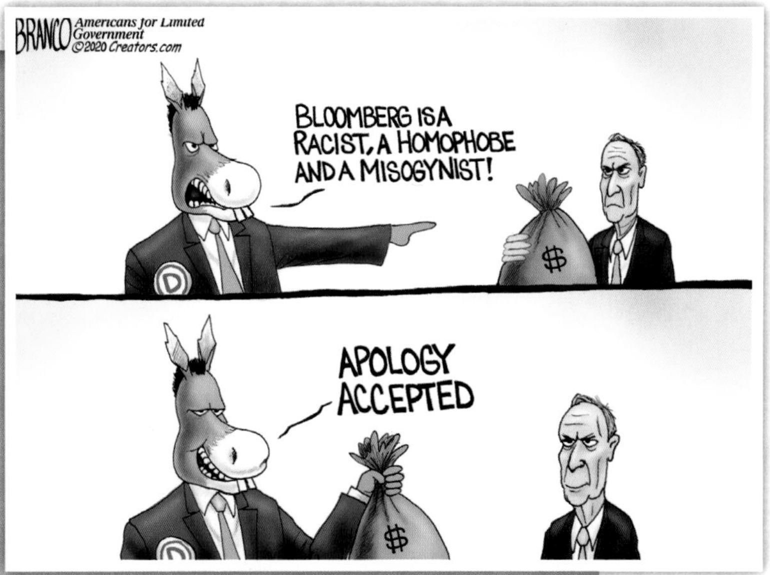
BRANCO Americans for Limited Government ©2020 Creators.com
BLOOMBERG IS A RACIST, A HOMOPHOBE AND A MISOGYNIST!
$
APOLOGY ACCEPTED
$

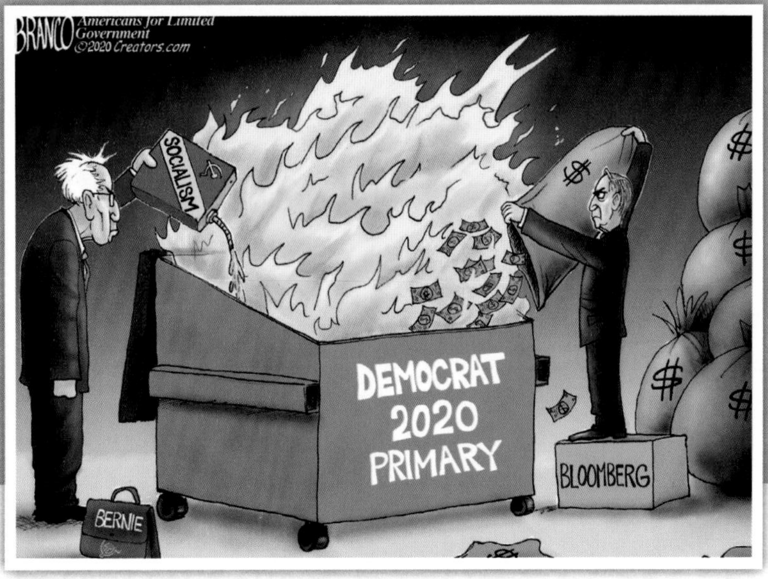
BRANCO Americans for Limited Government ©2020 Creators.com
SOCIALISM
DEMOCRAT 2020 PRIMARY
BLOOMBERG
BERNIE

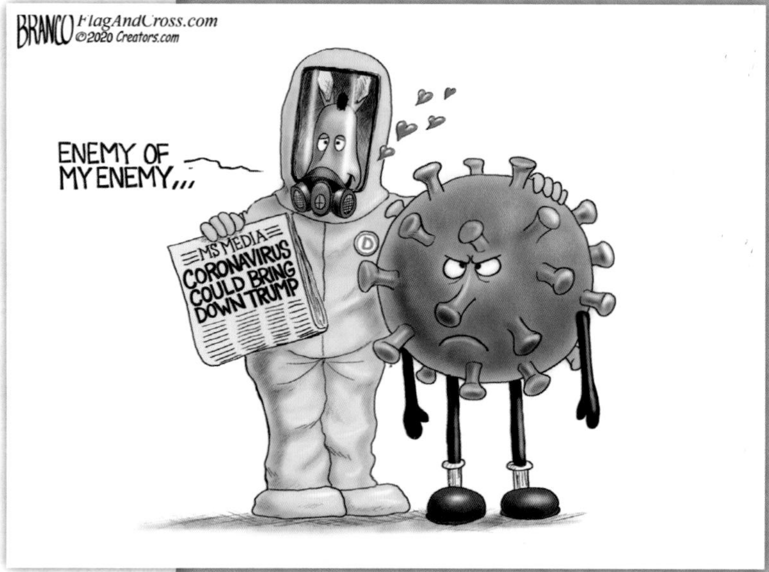
BRANCO FlagAndCross.com ©2020 Creators.com
ENEMY OF MY ENEMY...
MS MEDIA
CORONAVIRUS COULD BRING DOWN TRUMP

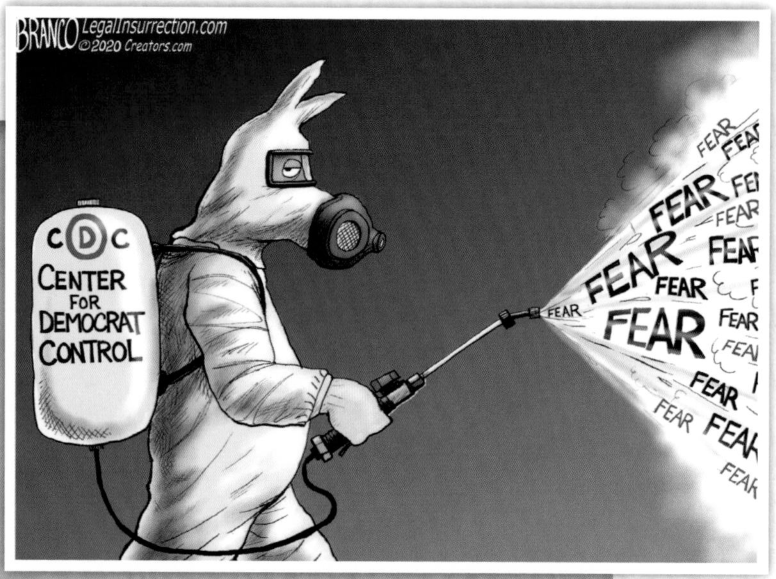
BRANCO LegalInsurrection.com ©2020 Creators.com
CDC
CENTER FOR DEMOCRAT CONTROL
FEAR FEAR FEAR FEAR FEAR FEAR

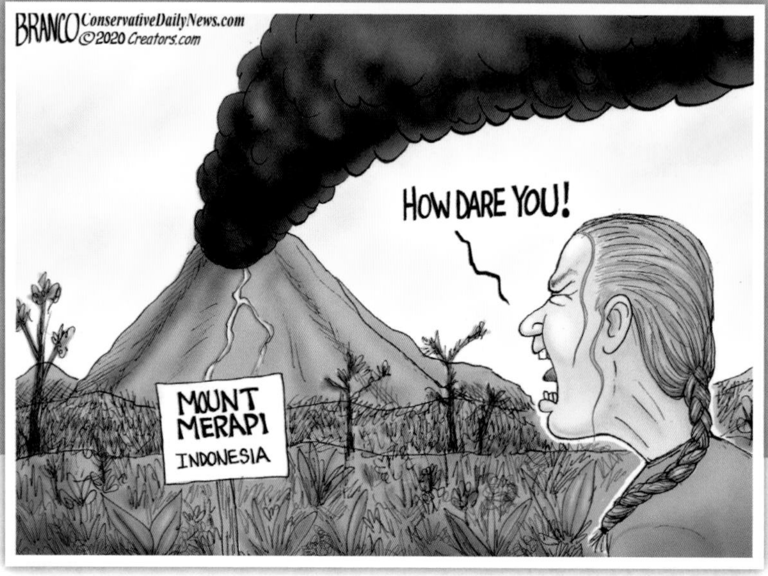
BRANCO ConservativeDailyNews.com ©2020 Creators.com
HOW DARE YOU!
MOUNT MERAPI
INDONESIA

BRANCO FlagAndCross.com
©2020 Creators.com
STOCK MARKET
CORONAVIRUS
YES!
MS MEDIA

BRANCO LegalInsurrection.com
©2020 Creators.com
BIDEN 2020
BECAUSE TRUMP IS JUST TOO EMBARRASSING
I GOT HAIRY LEGS
NEVER TRUMPER
BIDEN 2020

BRANCO Americans for Limited Government
©2020 Creators.com
MONSTERS
PANIC
COVID-19

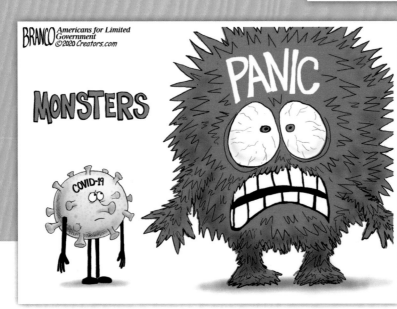

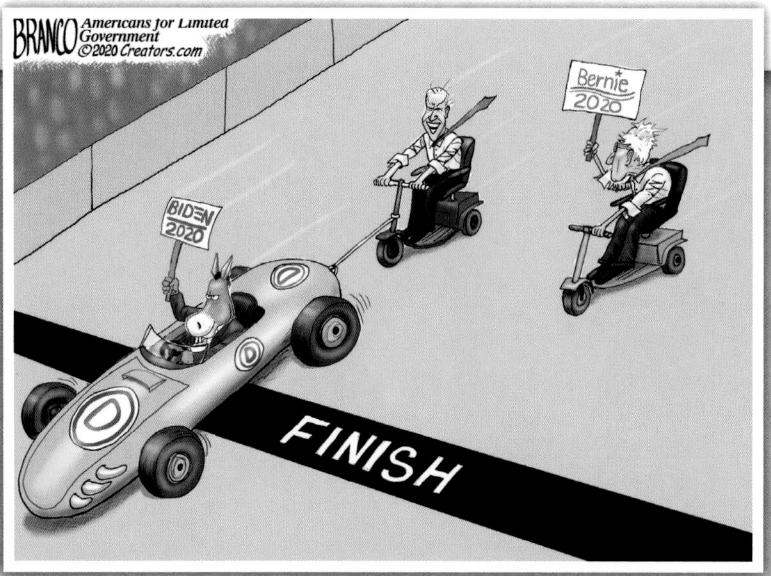
BRANCO Americans for Limited Government ©2020 Creators.com
Bernie 2020
BIDEN 2020
FINISH

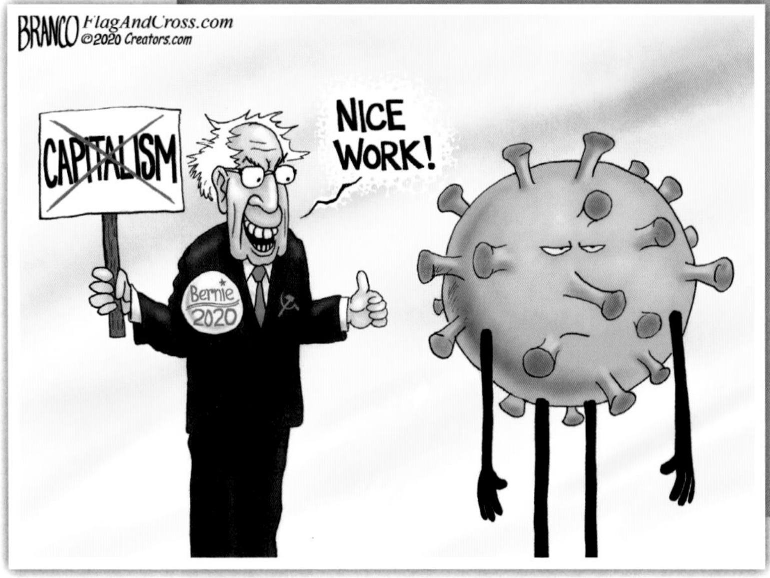
BRANCO FlagAndCross.com ©2020 Creators.com
CAPITALISM
NICE WORK!
Bernie 2020

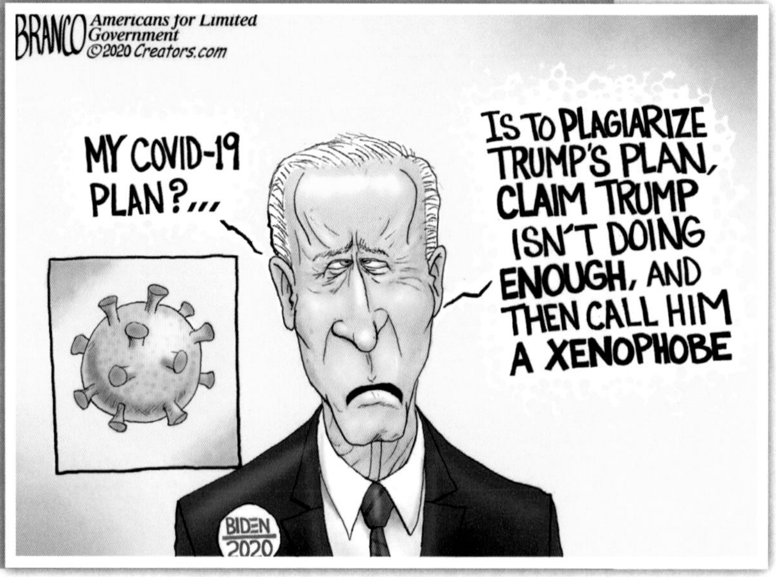
BRANCO Americans for Limited Government ©2020 Creators.com
MY COVID-19 PLAN?...
IS TO PLAGIARIZE TRUMP'S PLAN, CLAIM TRUMP ISN'T DOING ENOUGH, AND THEN CALL HIM A XENOPHOBE
BIDEN 2020

BRANCO ConservativeDailyNews.com ©2020 Creators.com
WUHAN-CORONAVIRUS
IT WASN'T ME

BRANCO Americans for Limited Government ©2020 Creators.com
COVID-19 FINANCIAL CRISIS
RESCUE AID

BRANCO FlagAndCross.com ©2020 Creators.com
MAINSTREAM MEDIA NEWS
TRUMP'S FAULT

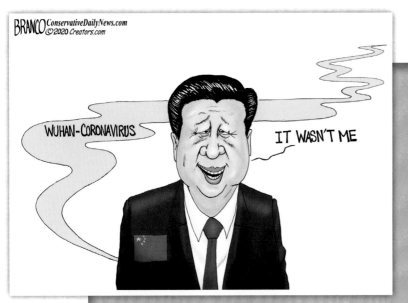

BRANCO ConservativeDailyNews.com
©2020 Creators.com
NADLER

BRANCO FlagAndCross.com
©2020 Creators.com
MY MAIN PRIORITY IS THE LIVES OF THE AMERICAN PEOPLE
CNN
WORD PROCESSOR
I WANT PEOPLE TO DIE TO SAVE THE ECONOMY

BRANCO LegalInsurrection.com
©2020 Creators.com
THE EMPEROR'S NEW CLOTHES
Mainstream Media
TRUMP'S FAULT

BRANCO Americans for Limited Government ©2020 Creators.com
CORONAVIRUS RELATED TRUMP DERANGEMENT SYNDROME
TRUMP ORDERS USNS COMFORT TO NEW YORK
COMFORT
TRUMP ORDERS EARLY TRAVEL BAN FROM CHINA THAT SAVED 1000'S OF LIVES
TRUMP PUSHES FOR ANTI-MALARIA DRUGS PROVING TO BE BEST BET AGAINST COVID-19
TRUMP FAST TRACKED VENTILATORS AND MEDICAL MASKS PRODUCTION
TRUMP DERANGMENT SYNDROME
TRUMP DERANGMENT SYNDROME
TRUMP CAN NOT DO ANYTHING RIGHT!!!
MAINSTREAM MEDIA

BRANCO LegalInsurrection.com ©2020 Creators.com
THE CURE IS KILLING HIM
I KNOW, ISN'T IT AWFUL
ECONOMIC SHUTDOWN

BRANCO ConservativeDailyNews.com ©2020 Creators.com
ASH HEAP OF HISTORY
Bernie 2020
MODERATE DEMOCRAT
SOVIET UNION

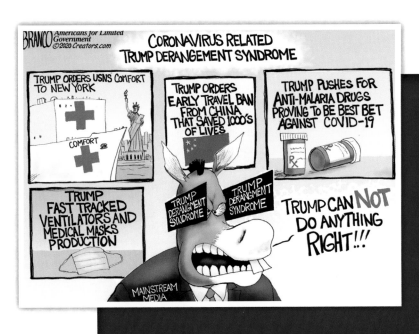

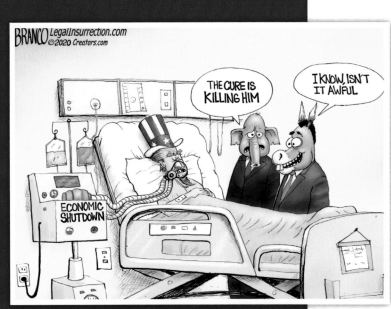

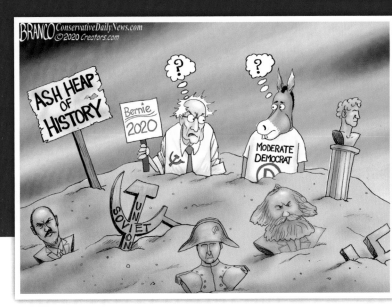

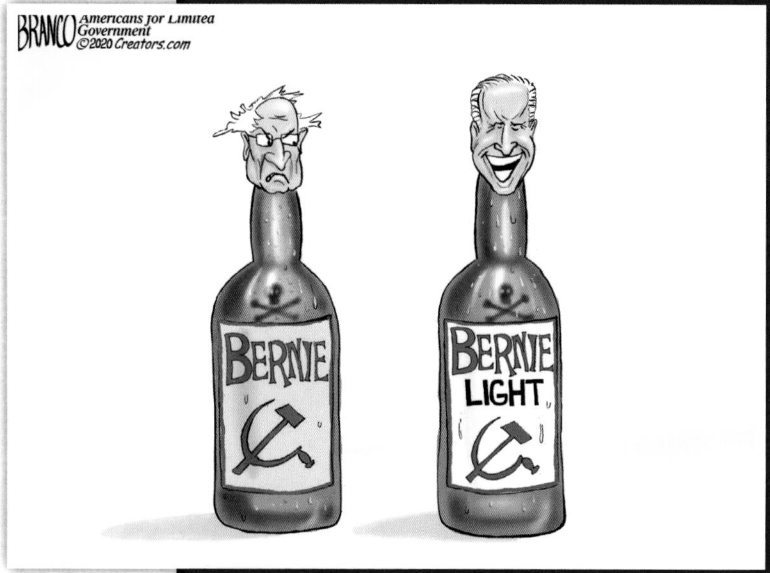
BRANCO Americans for Limited Government ©2020 Creators.com
BERNIE
BERNIE LIGHT

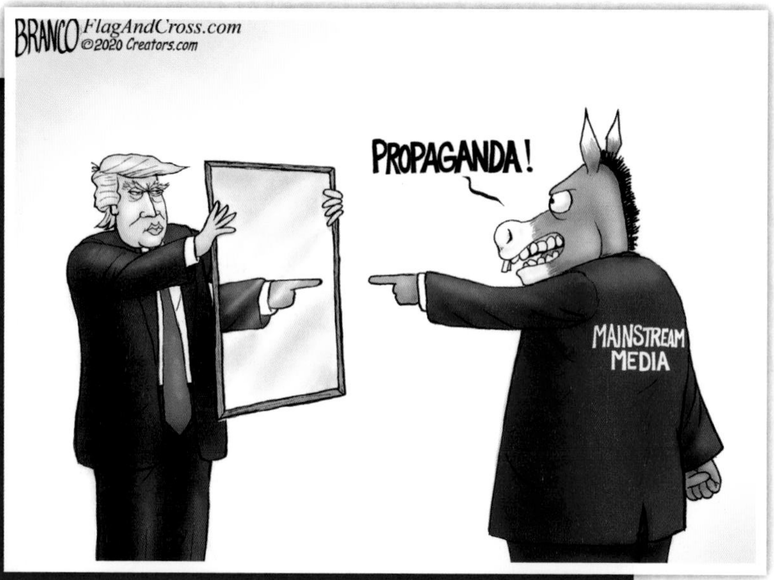
BRANCO FlagAndCross.com ©2020 Creators.com
PROPAGANDA!
MAINSTREAM MEDIA

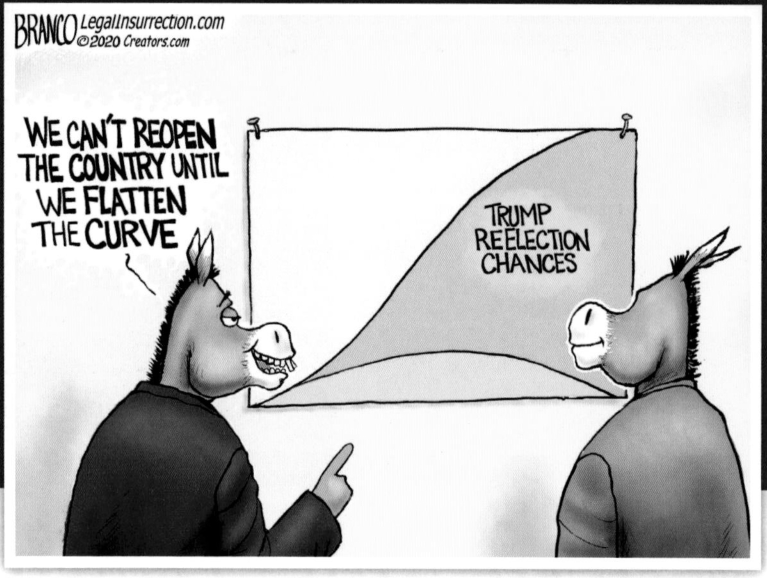
BRANCO LegalInsurrection.com ©2020 Creators.com
WE CAN'T REOPEN THE COUNTRY UNTIL WE FLATTEN THE CURVE
TRUMP REELECTION CHANCES

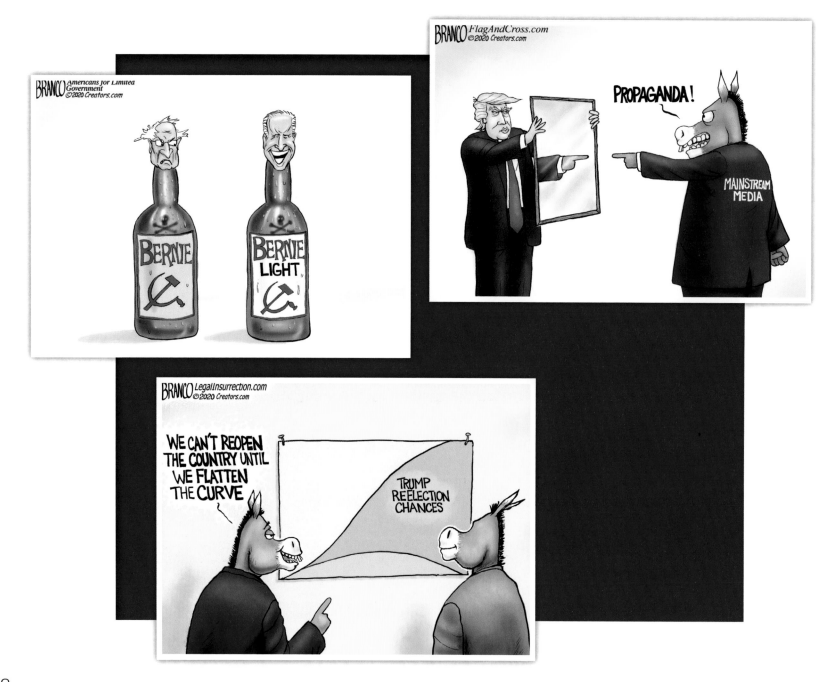

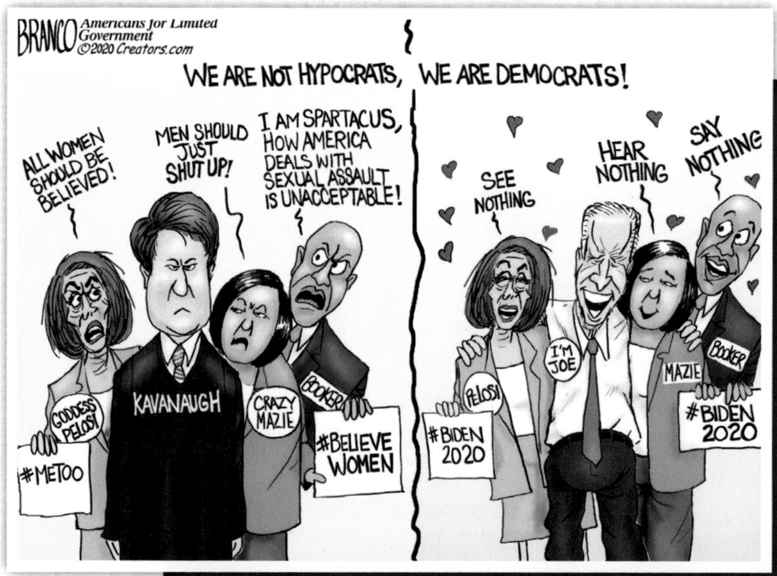
BRANCO Americans for Limited Government ©2020 Creators.com
WE ARE NOT HYPOCRATS, WE ARE DEMOCRATS!
ALL WOMEN SHOULD BE BELIEVED!
MEN SHOULD JUST SHUT UP!
I AM SPARTACUS, HOW AMERICA DEALS WITH SEXUAL ASSAULT IS UNACCEPTABLE!
GODDESS PELOSI
#METOO
KAVANAUGH
CRAZY MAZIE
BOOKER
#BELIEVE WOMEN
SEE NOTHING
HEAR NOTHING
SAY NOTHING
PELOSI
#BIDEN 2020
I'M JOE
MAZIE
BOOKER
#BIDEN 2020

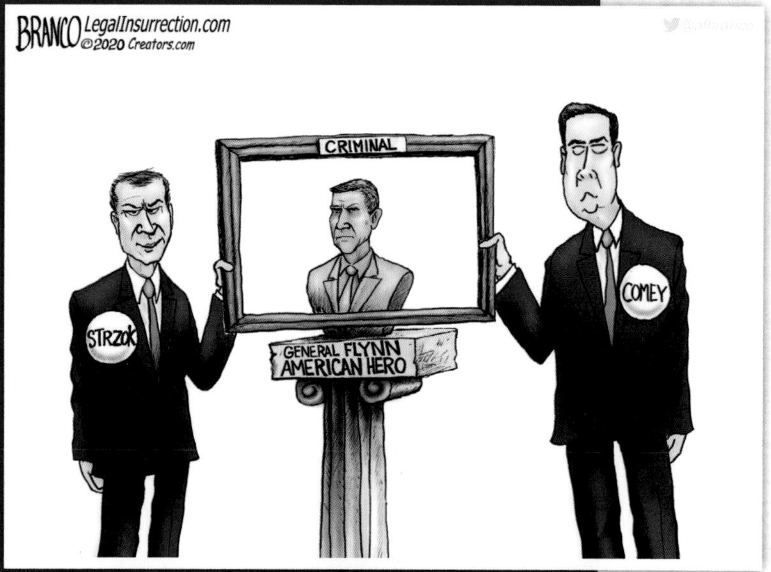
BRANCO LegalInsurrection.com ©2020 Creators.com
CRIMINAL
STRZOK
GENERAL FLYNN AMERICAN HERO
COMEY

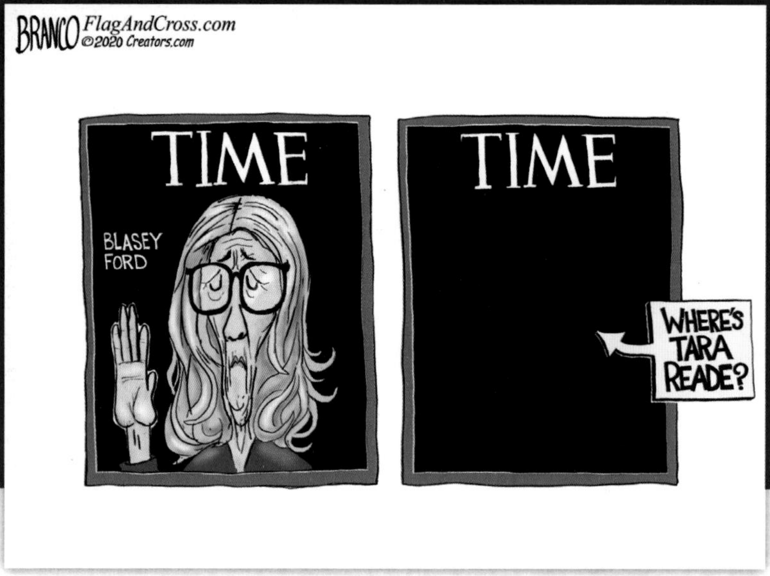
BRANCO FlagAndCross.com ©2020 Creators.com
TIME
BLASEY FORD
TIME
WHERE'S TARA READE?

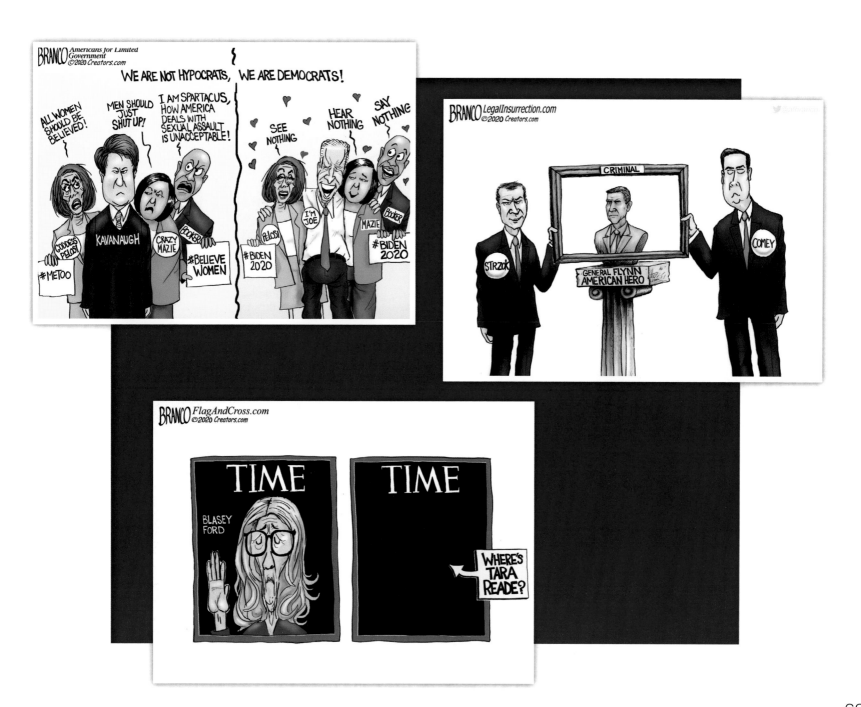

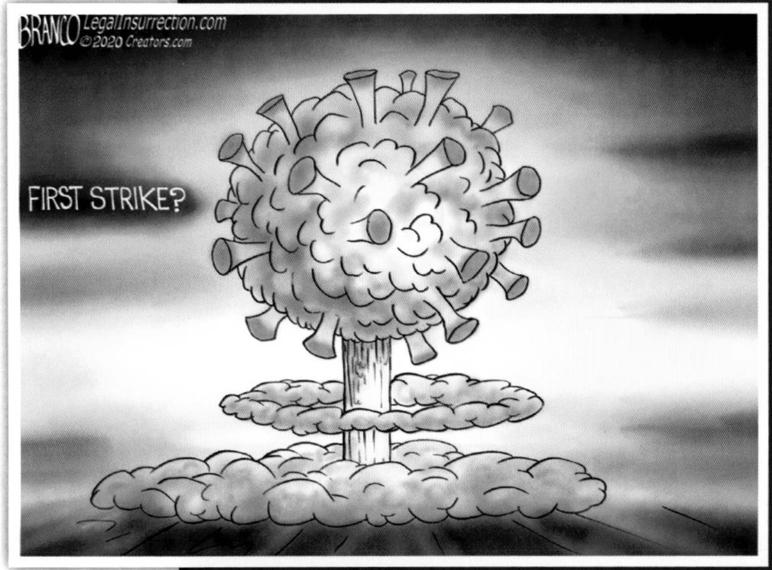
BRANCO LegalInsurrection.com ©2020 Creators.com
FIRST STRIKE?

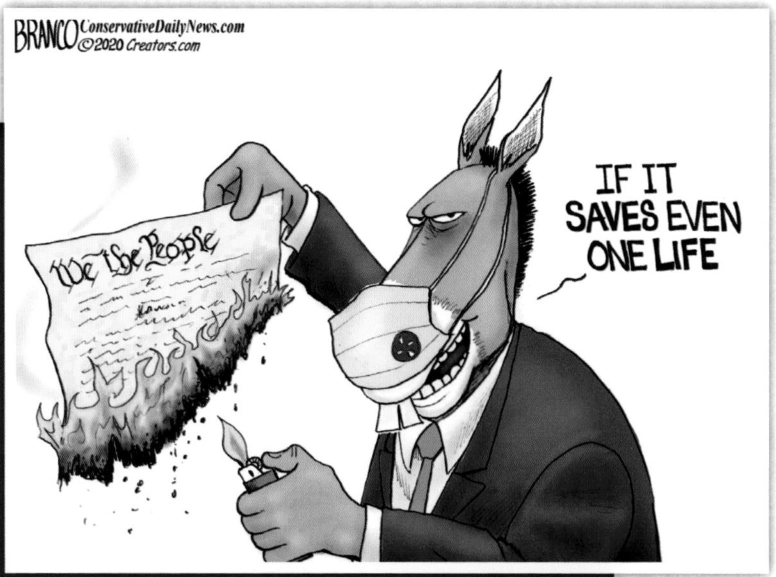
BRANCO ConservativeDailyNews.com ©2020 Creators.com
We the People
IF IT SAVES EVEN ONE LIFE

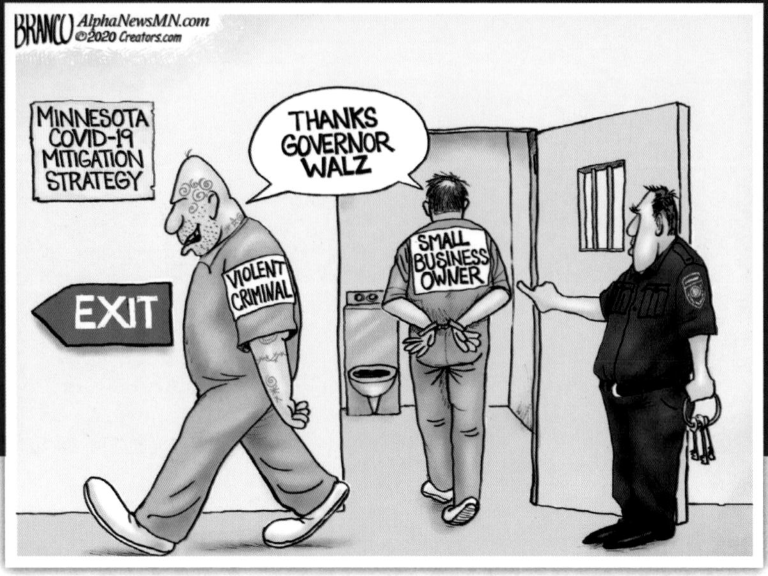
BRANCO AlphaNewsMN.com ©2020 Creators.com
MINNESOTA COVID-19 MITIGATION STRATEGY
THANKS GOVERNOR WALZ
VIOLENT CRIMINAL
SMALL BUSINESS OWNER
EXIT

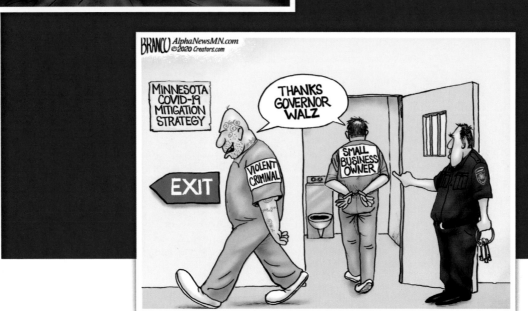

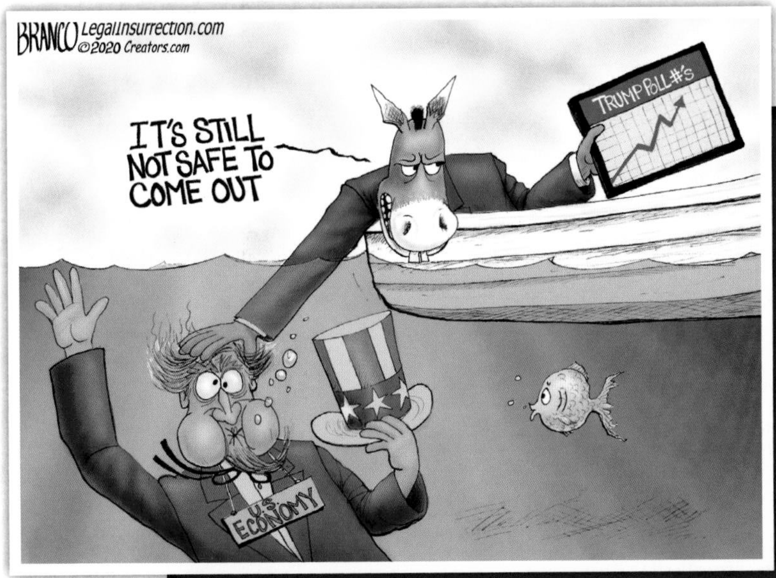
BRANCO LegalInsurrection.com
©2020 Creators.com
IT'S STILL NOT SAFE TO COME OUT
TRUMP POLL #'s
U.S. ECONOMY

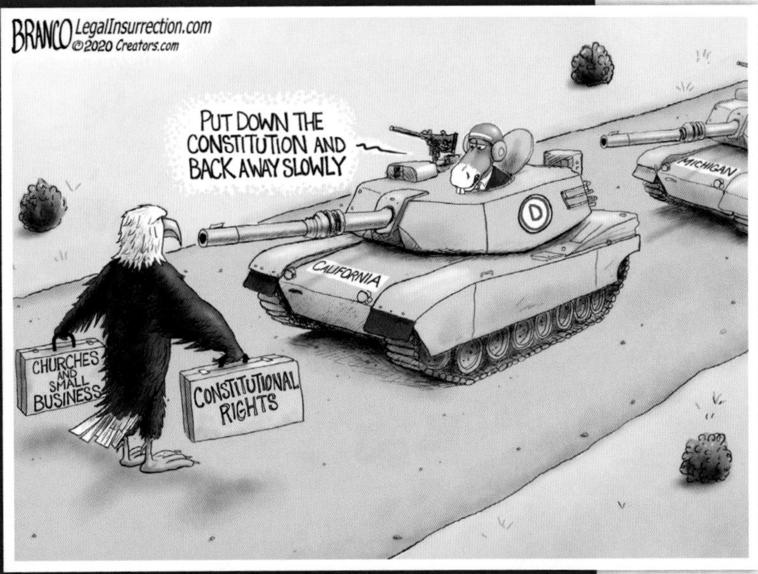
BRANCO LegalInsurrection.com
©2020 Creators.com
PUT DOWN THE CONSTITUTION AND BACK AWAY SLOWLY
D
CALIFORNIA
MICHIGAN
CHURCHES AND SMALL BUSINESS
CONSTITUTIONAL RIGHTS

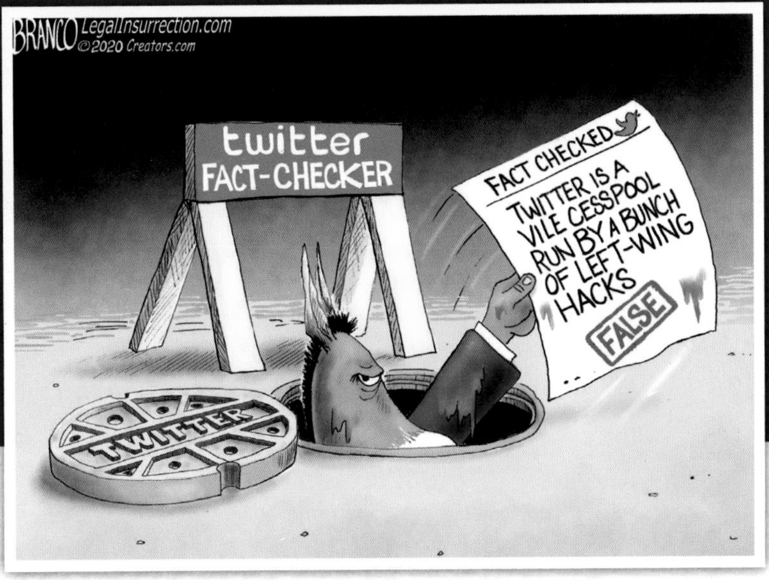
BRANCO LegalInsurrection.com
©2020 Creators.com
twitter
FACT-CHECKER
FACT CHECKED
TWITTER IS A VILE CESSPOOL RUN BY A BUNCH OF LEFT-WING HACKS
FALSE
TWITTER

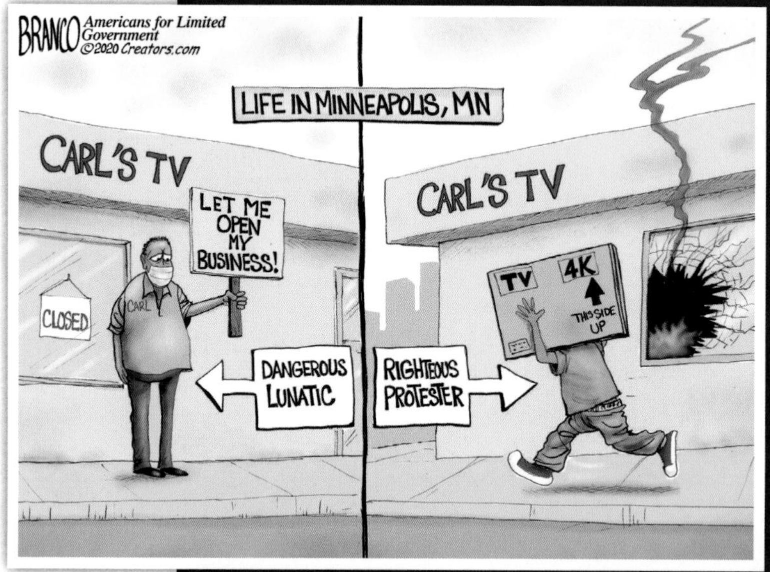
BRANCO Americans for Limited Government ©2020 Creators.com
LIFE IN MINNEAPOLIS, MN
CARL'S TV
LET ME OPEN MY BUSINESS!
CLOSED
CARL
DANGEROUS LUNATIC
CARL'S TV
TV
4K
THIS SIDE UP
RIGHTEOUS PROTESTER

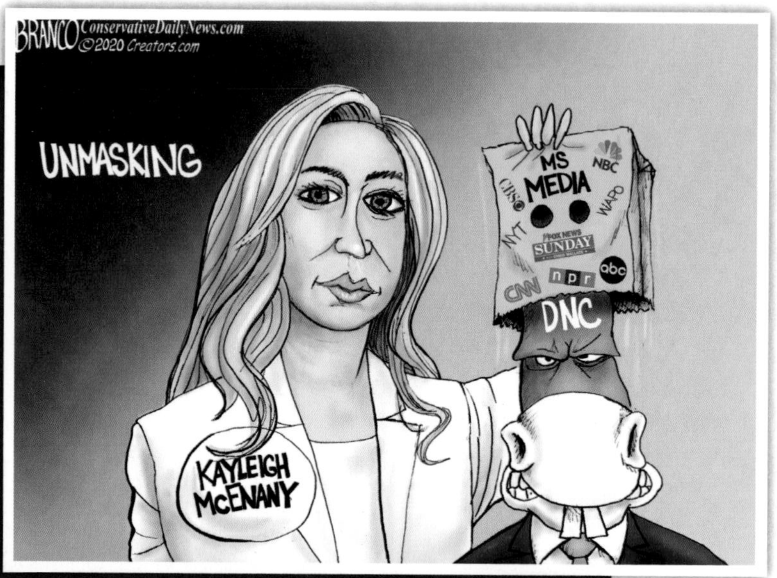
BRANCO ConservativeDailyNews.com ©2020 Creators.com
UNMASKING
KAYLEIGH McENANY
MS MEDIA
NBC
CBS
WAPO
NYT
FOX NEWS SUNDAY
CNN
npr
abc
DNC

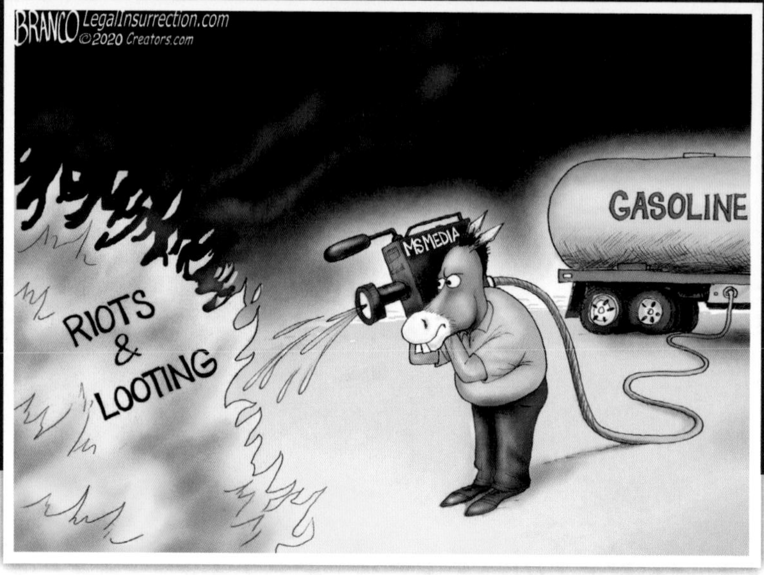
BRANCO LegalInsurrection.com ©2020 Creators.com
RIOTS & LOOTING
MSMEDIA
GASOLINE

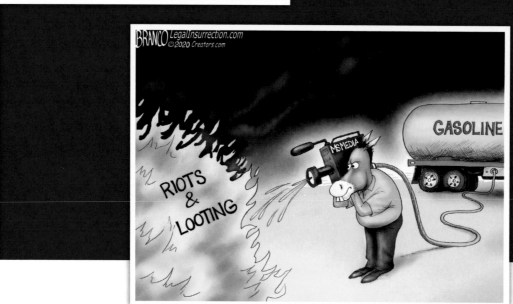

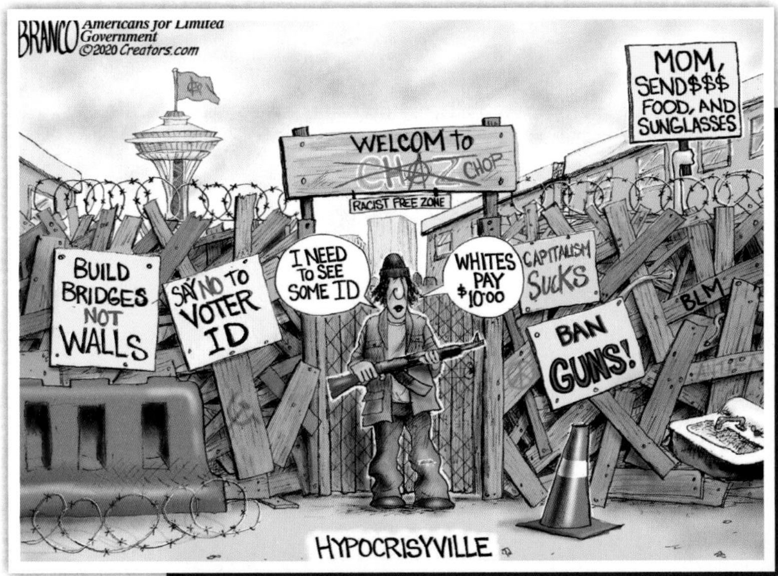
BRANCO Americans for Limited Government ©2020 Creators.com
MOM, SEND $$$ FOOD, AND SUNGLASSES
WELCOM to CHAZ CHOP
RACIST FREE ZONE
BUILD BRIDGES NOT WALLS
SAY NO TO VOTER ID
I NEED TO SEE SOME ID
WHITES PAY $10.00
CAPITALISM SUCKS
BLM
BAN GUNS!
HYPOCRISYVILLE

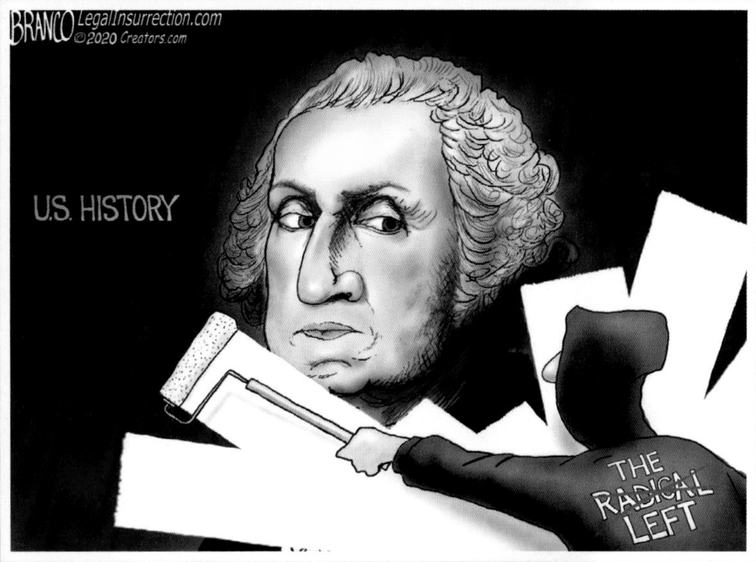
BRANCO LegalInsurrection.com ©2020 Creators.com
U.S. HISTORY
THE RADICAL LEFT

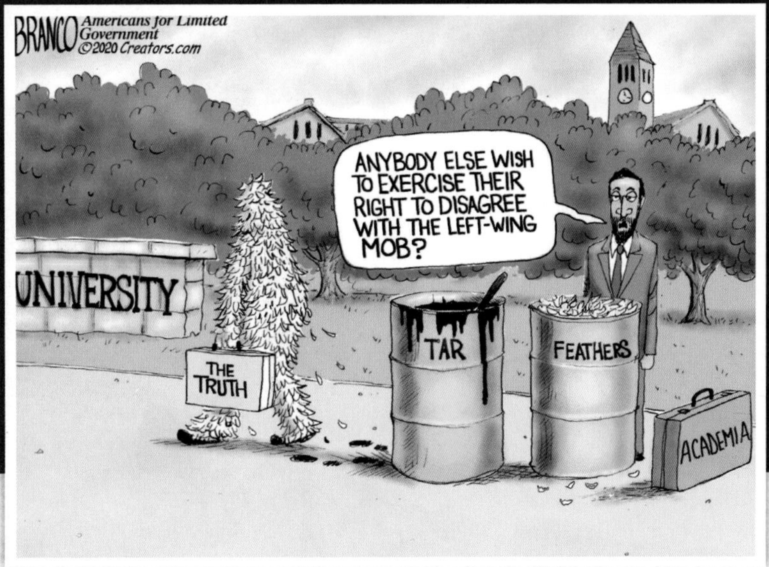
BRANCO Americans for Limited Government ©2020 Creators.com
ANYBODY ELSE WISH TO EXERCISE THEIR RIGHT TO DISAGREE WITH THE LEFT-WING MOB?
UNIVERSITY
TAR
FEATHERS
THE TRUTH
ACADEMIA

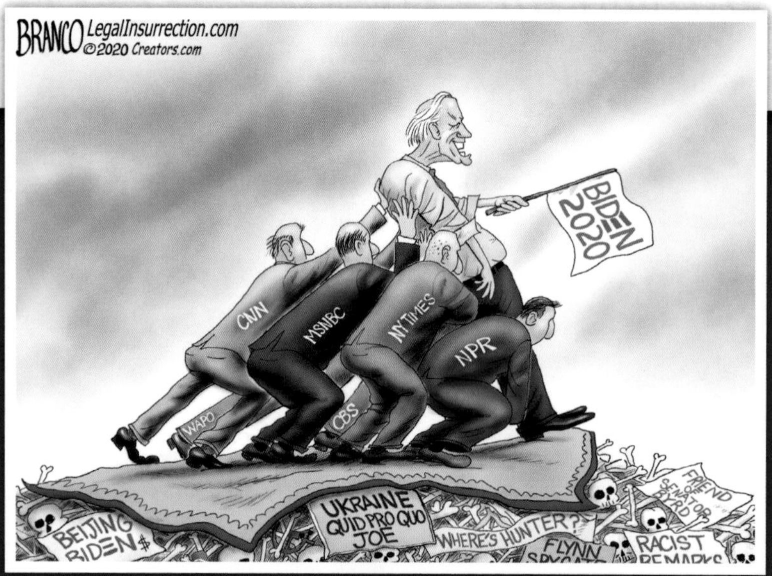
BRANCO LegalInsurrection.com
©2020 Creators.com
BIDEN 2020
CNN
MSNBC
NYTIMES
NPR
WAPO
CBS
UKRAINE QUID PRO QUO JOE
BEIJING BIDEN$
WHERE'S HUNTER?
FLYNN
RACIST

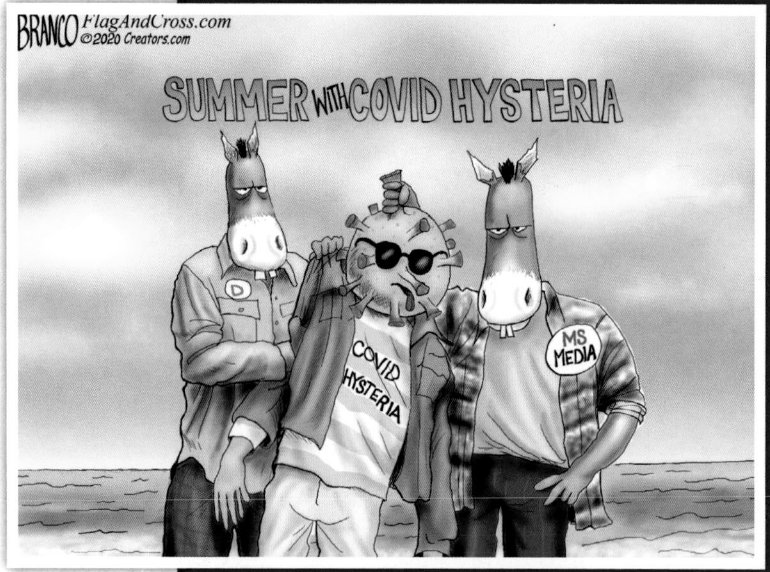
BRANCO FlagAndCross.com
©2020 Creators.com
SUMMER WITH COVID HYSTERIA
D
COVID HYSTERIA
MS MEDIA

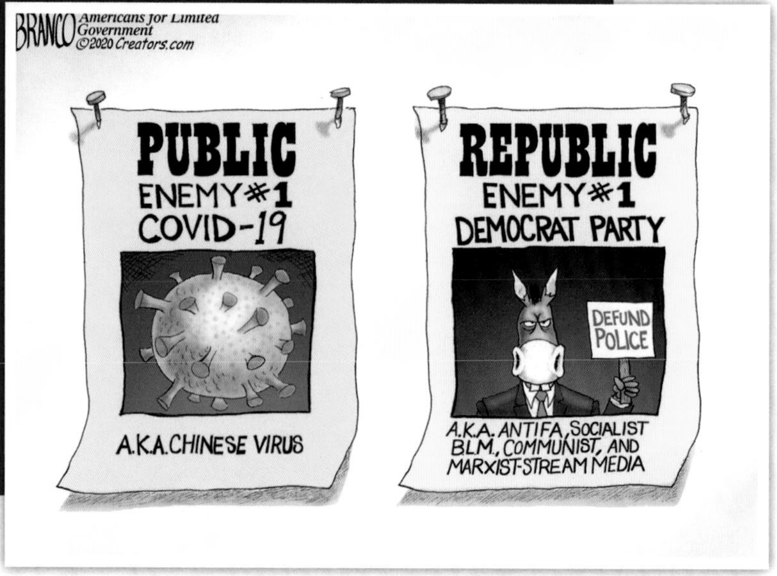
BRANCO Americans for Limited Government
©2020 Creators.com
PUBLIC
ENEMY #1
COVID-19
A.K.A. CHINESE VIRUS
REPUBLIC
ENEMY #1
DEMOCRAT PARTY
DEFUND POLICE
A.K.A. ANTIFA, SOCIALIST BLM, COMMUNIST, AND MARXIST-STREAM MEDIA

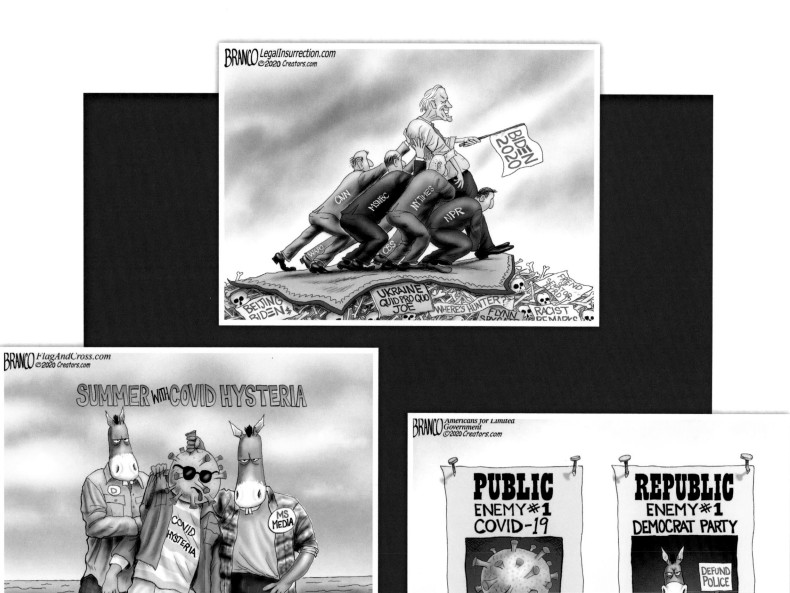

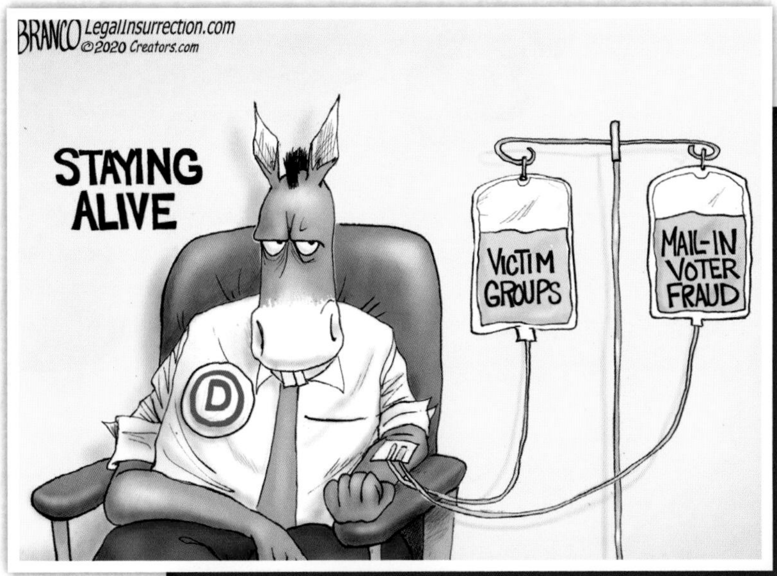
BRANCO LegalInsurrection.com
©2020 Creators.com
STAYING ALIVE
VICTIM GROUPS
MAIL-IN VOTER FRAUD
D

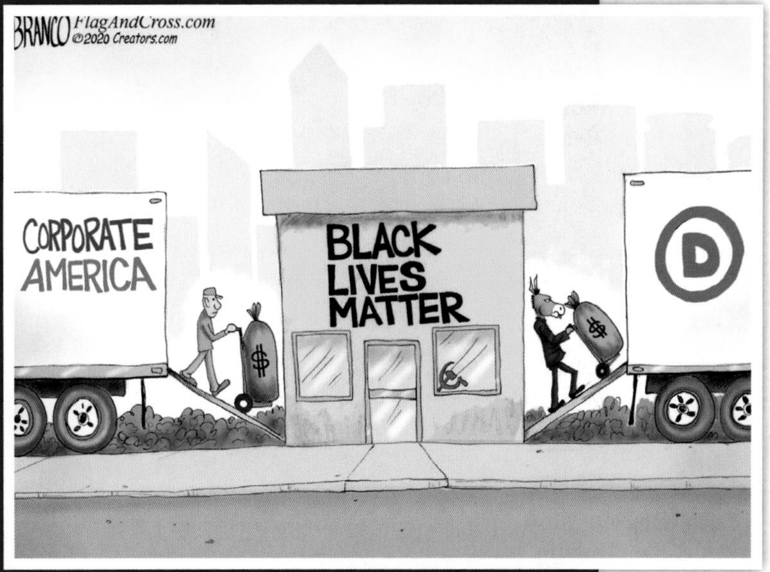
BRANCO FlagAndCross.com
©2020 Creators.com
CORPORATE AMERICA
BLACK LIVES MATTER
D
$

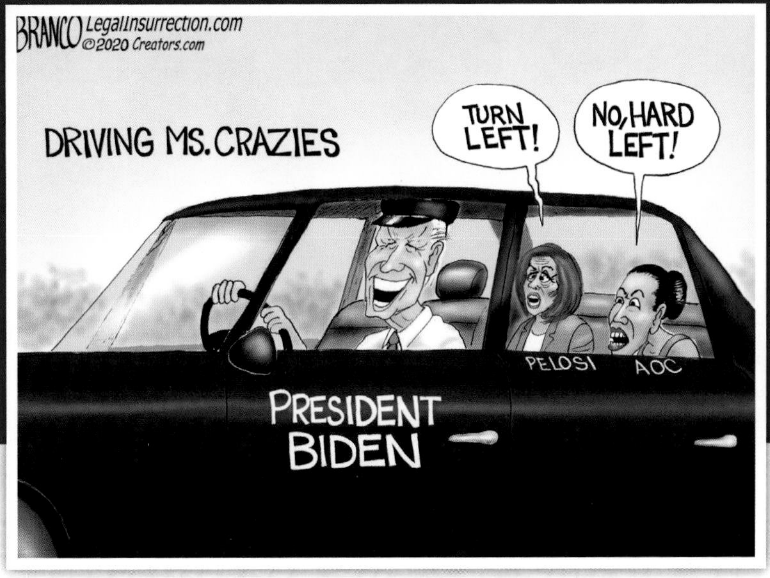
BRANCO LegalInsurrection.com
©2020 Creators.com
DRIVING MS. CRAZIES
TURN LEFT!
NO, HARD LEFT!
PELOSI
AOC
PRESIDENT BIDEN

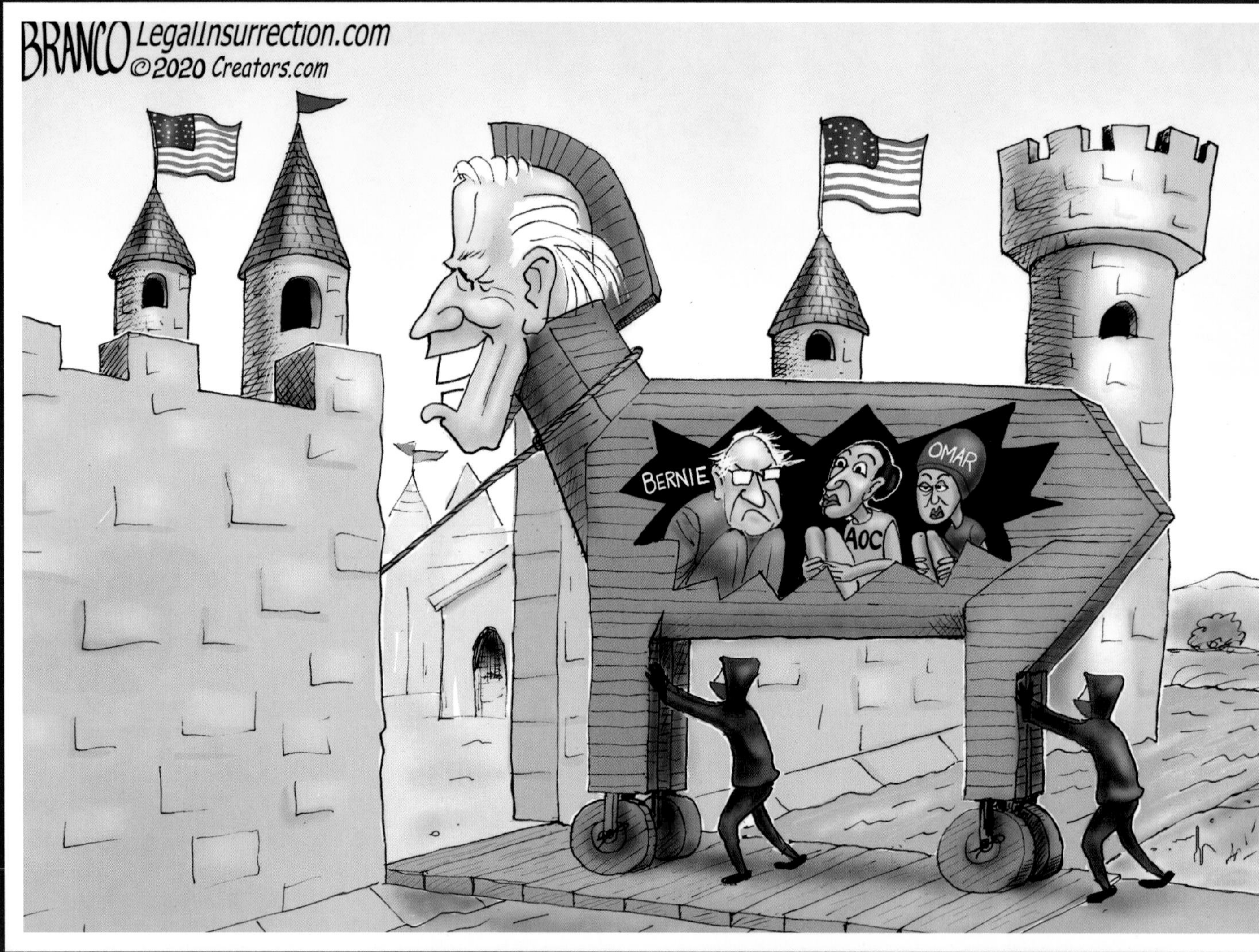
BRANCO LegalInsurrection.com
©2020 Creators.com
BERNIE
AOC
OMAR

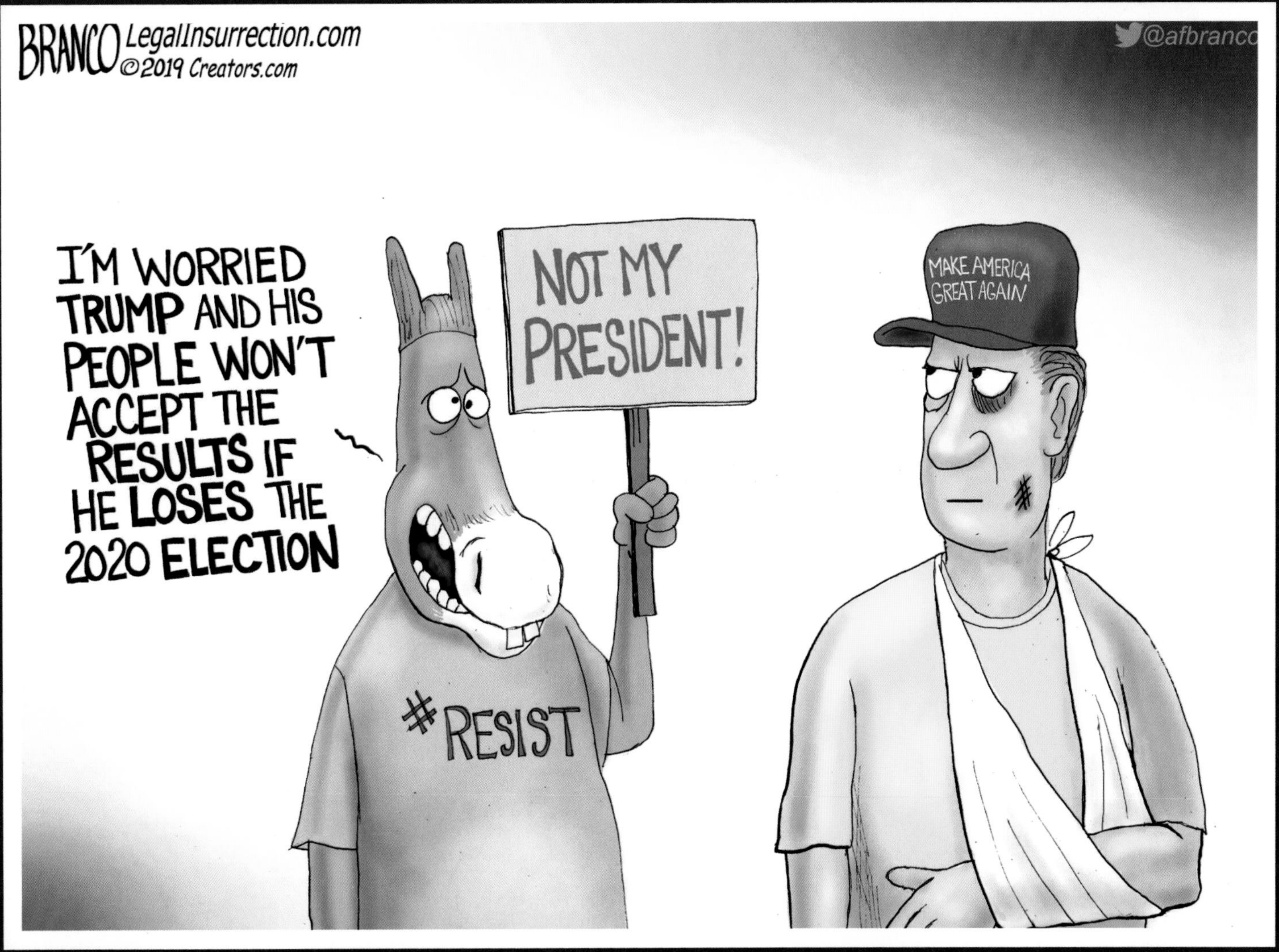
BRANCO LegalInsurrection.com ©2019 Creators.com
@afbranco
I'M WORRIED TRUMP AND HIS PEOPLE WON'T ACCEPT THE RESULTS IF HE LOSES THE 2020 ELECTION
NOT MY PRESIDENT!
#RESIST
MAKE AMERICA GREAT AGAIN

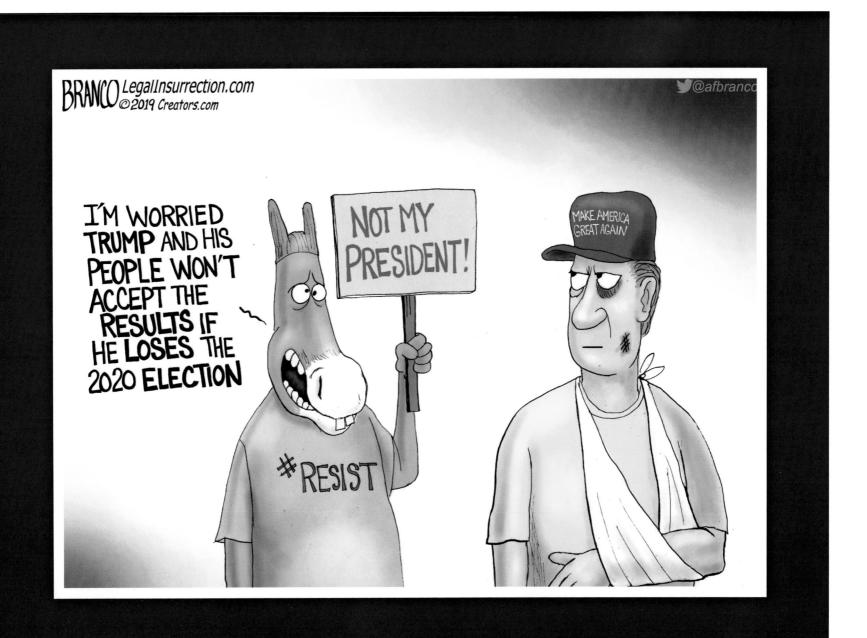

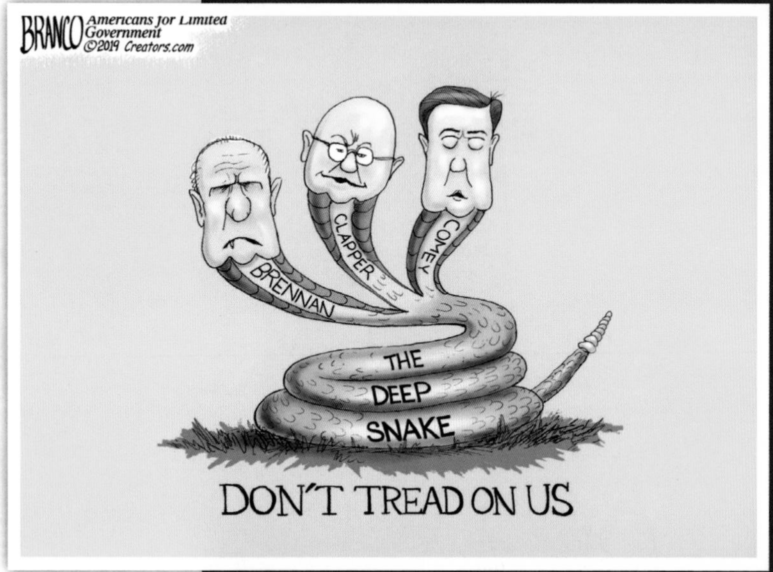
BRANCO Americans for Limited Government ©2019 Creators.com
BRENNAN
CLAPPER
COMEY
THE DEEP SNAKE
DON'T TREAD ON US

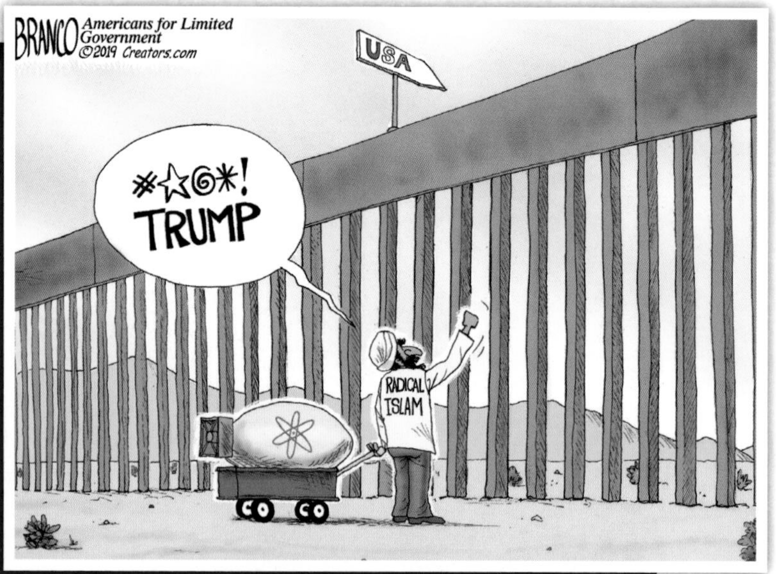
BRANCO Americans for Limited Government ©2019 Creators.com
USA
☆@! TRUMP
RADICAL ISLAM

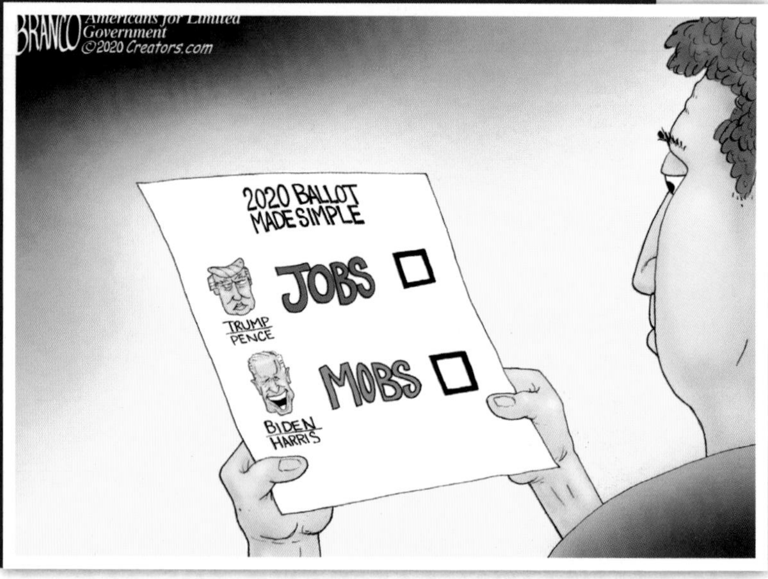
BRANCO Americans for Limited Government ©2020 Creators.com
2020 BALLOT MADE SIMPLE
JOBS
TRUMP PENCE
MOBS
BIDEN HARRIS

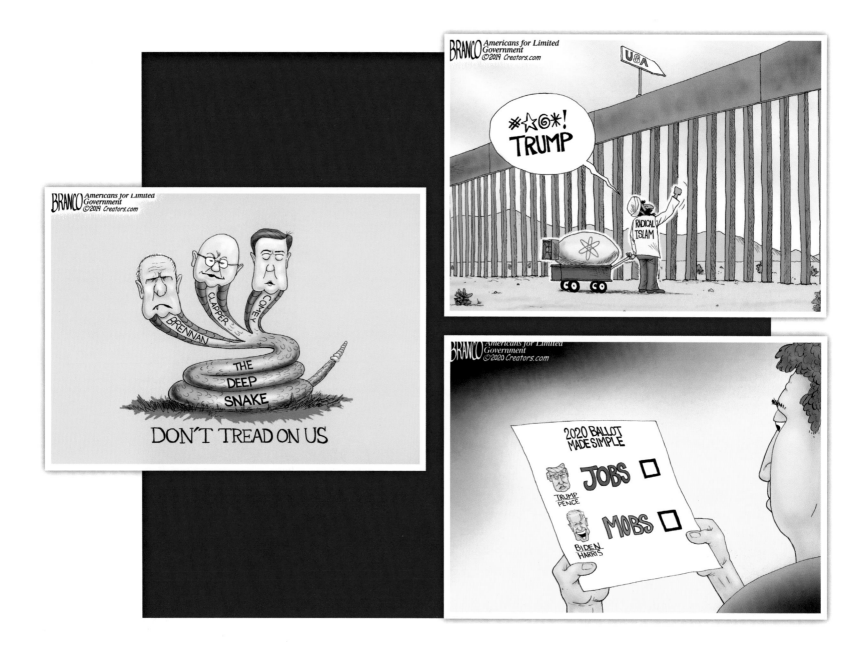

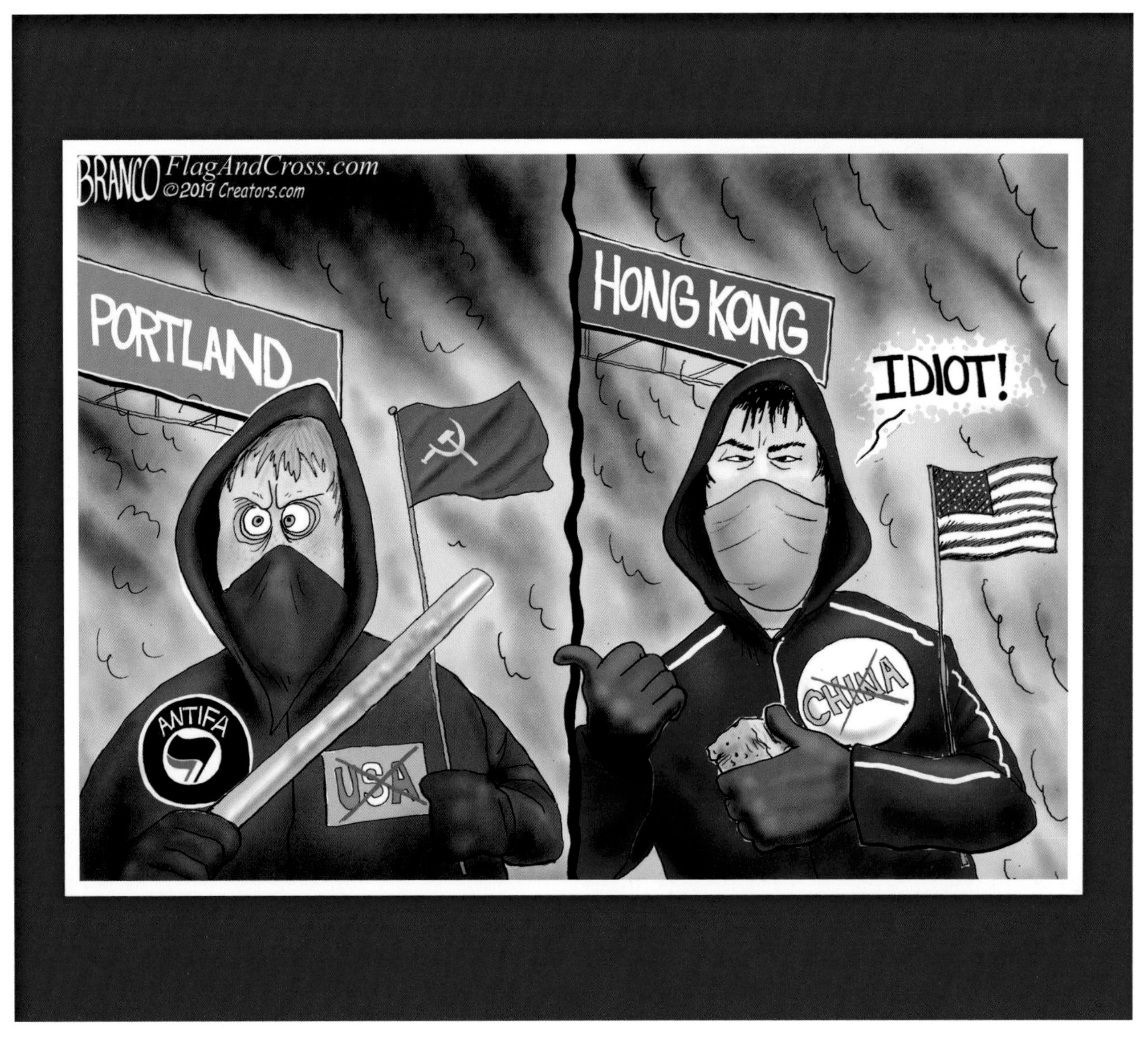
BRANCO FlagAndCross.com
©2019 Creators.com
PORTLAND
ANTIFA
USA
HONG KONG
IDIOT!
CHINA

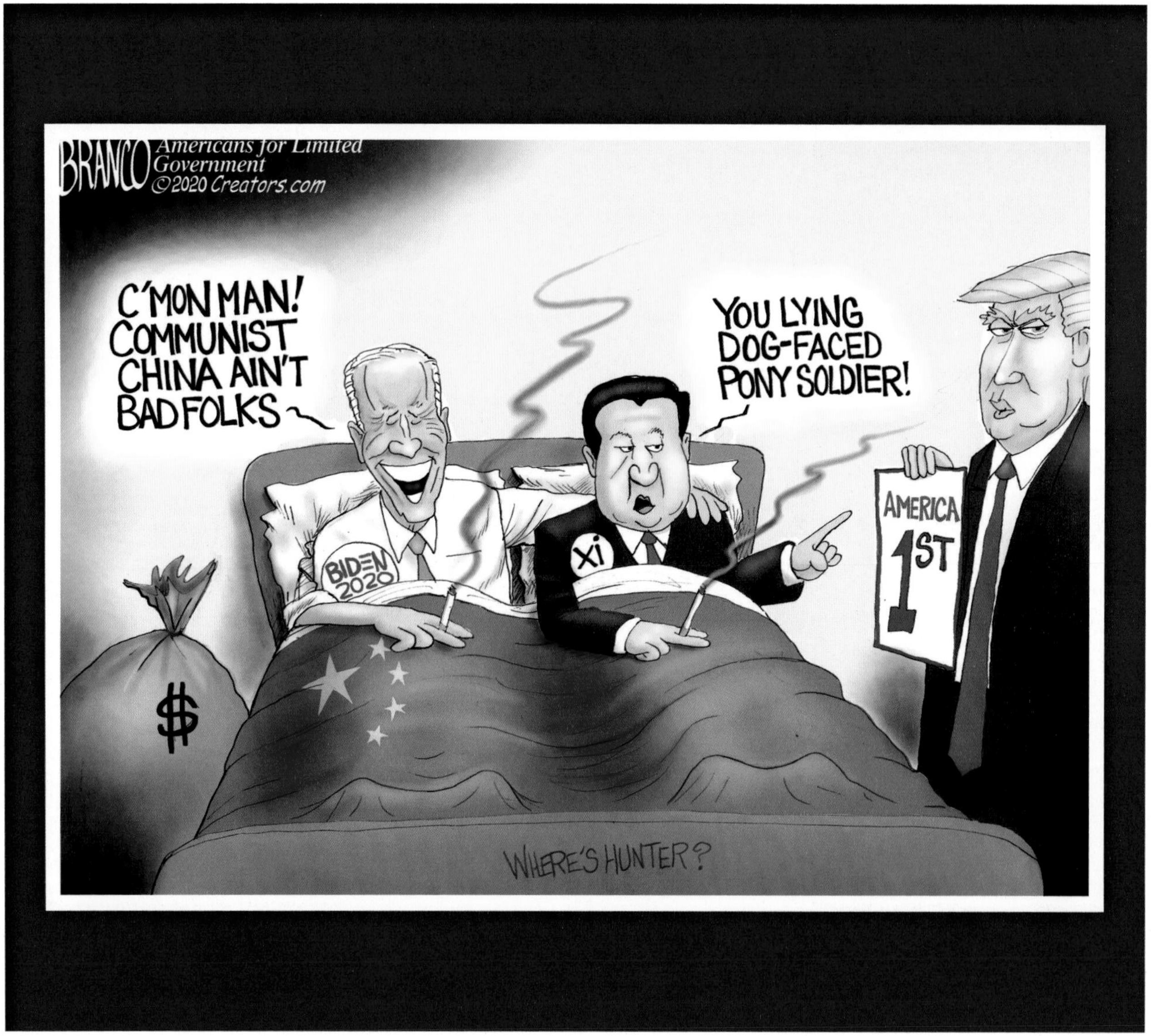
BRANCO Americans for Limited Government ©2020 Creators.com
C'MON MAN! COMMUNIST CHINA AIN'T BAD FOLKS
YOU LYING DOG-FACED PONY SOLDIER!
BIDEN 2020
Xi
AMERICA 1ST
$
WHERE'S HUNTER?

Hall of Fame

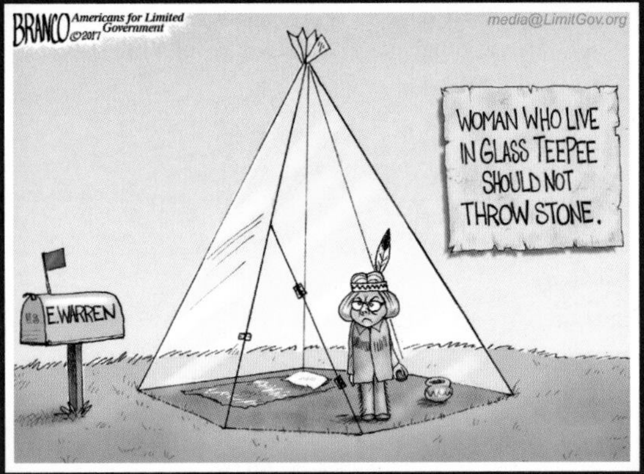
BRANCO Americans for Limited Government ©2017
media@LimitGov.org
WOMAN WHO LIVE IN GLASS TEEPEE SHOULD NOT THROW STONE.
E.WARREN

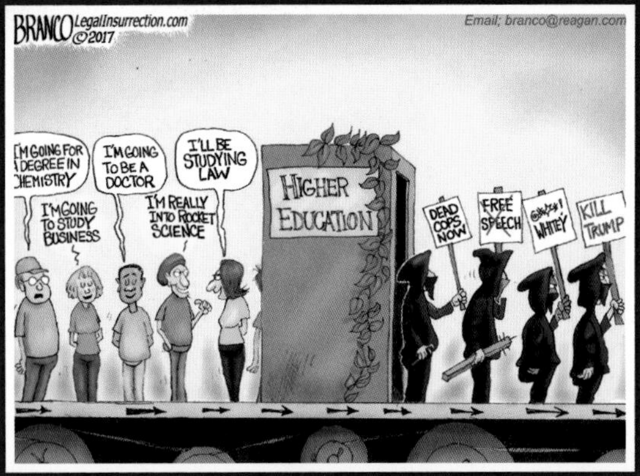
BRANCO LegalInsurrection.com ©2017
Email; branco@reagan.com
I'M GOING FOR A DEGREE IN CHEMISTRY
I'M GOING TO STUDY BUSINESS
I'M GOING TO BE A DOCTOR
I'M REALLY INTO ROCKET SCIENCE
I'LL BE STUDYING LAW
HIGHER EDUCATION
DEAD COPS NOW
FREE SPEECH
WHITEY
KILL TRUMP

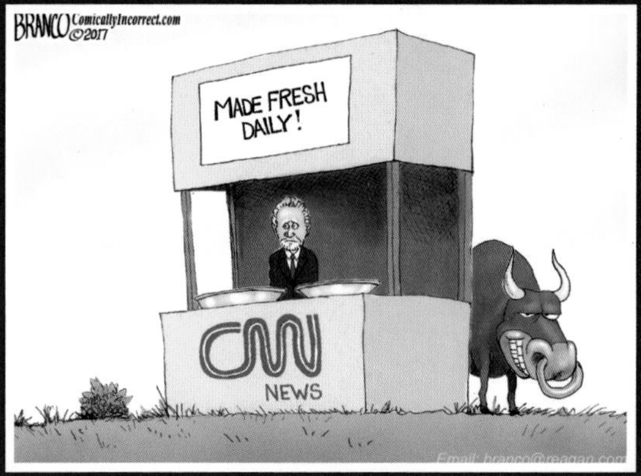
BRANCO ComicallyIncorrect.com ©2017
MADE FRESH DAILY!
CNN
NEWS

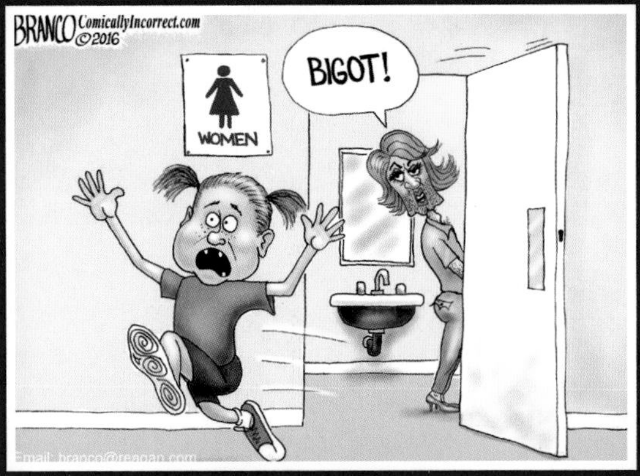
BRANCO ComicallyIncorrect.com ©2016
WOMEN
BIGOT!

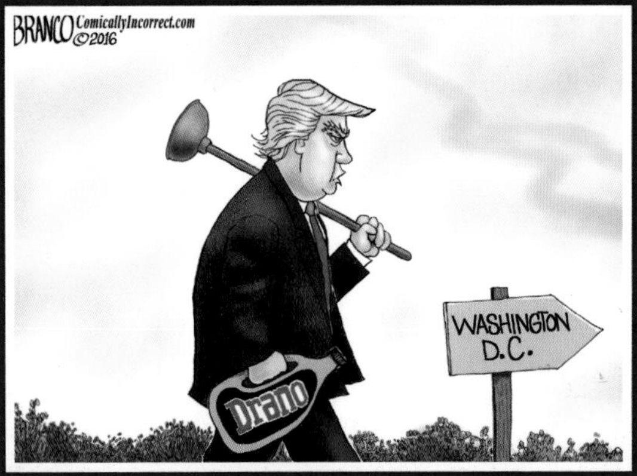
BRANCO ComicallyIncorrect.com ©2016
WASHINGTON D.C.
Drano

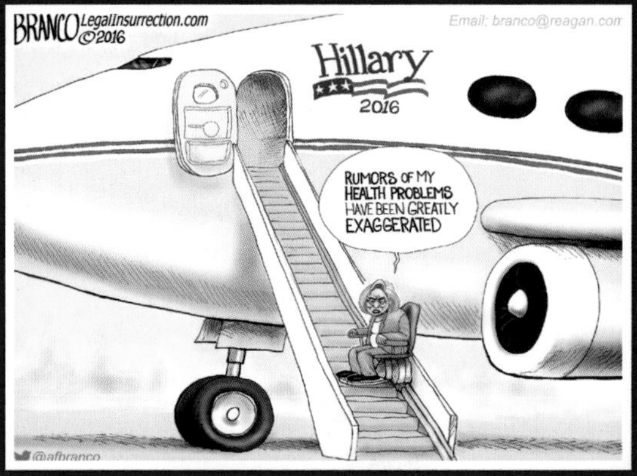
BRANCO LegalInsurrection.com ©2016
Email; branco@reagan.com
Hillary 2016
RUMORS OF MY HEALTH PROBLEMS HAVE BEEN GREATLY EXAGGERATED
@afbranco

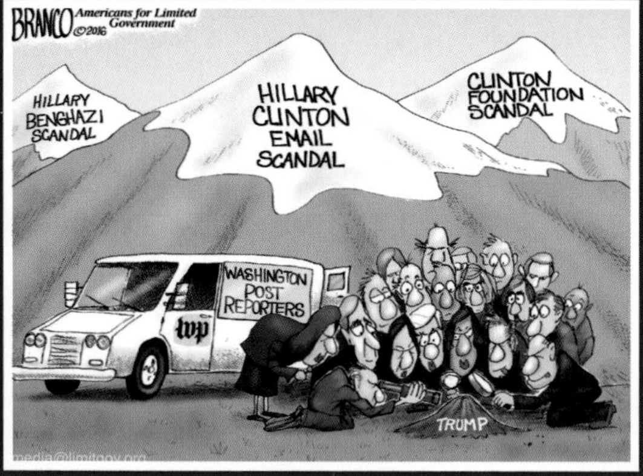
BRANCO Americans for Limited Government ©2016
HILLARY BENGHAZI SCANDAL
HILLARY CLINTON EMAIL SCANDAL
CLINTON FOUNDATION SCANDAL
WASHINGTON POST REPORTERS
wp
TRUMP

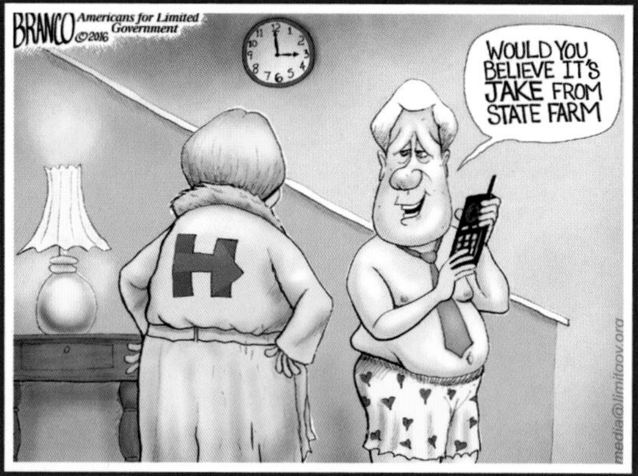
BRANCO Americans for Limited Government ©2016
WOULD YOU BELIEVE IT'S JAKE FROM STATE FARM
H

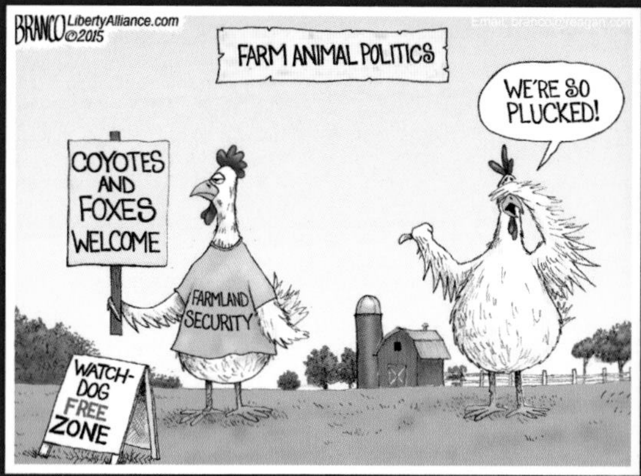
BRANCO LibertyAlliance.com ©2015
FARM ANIMAL POLITICS
WE'RE SO PLUCKED!
COYOTES AND FOXES WELCOME
FARMLAND SECURITY
WATCH-DOG FREE ZONE

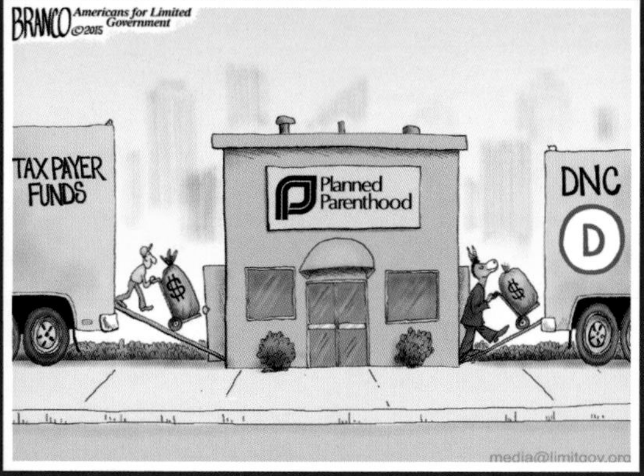
BRANCO Americans for Limited Government ©2015
TAX PAYER FUNDS
Planned Parenthood
DNC
D
media@limitgov.org

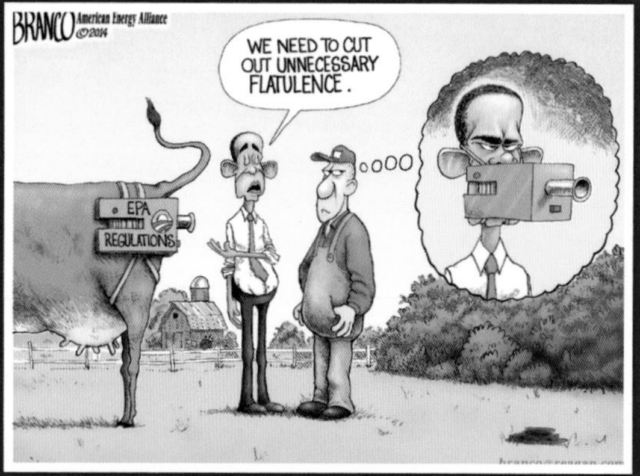
BRANCO American Energy Alliance ©2014
WE NEED TO CUT OUT UNNECESSARY FLATULENCE.
EPA REGULATIONS

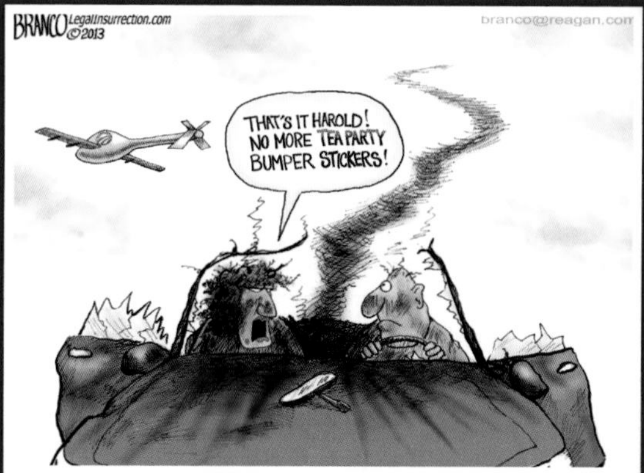
BRANCO LegalInsurrection.com ©2013
branco@reagan.com
THAT'S IT HAROLD! NO MORE TEA PARTY BUMPER STICKERS!

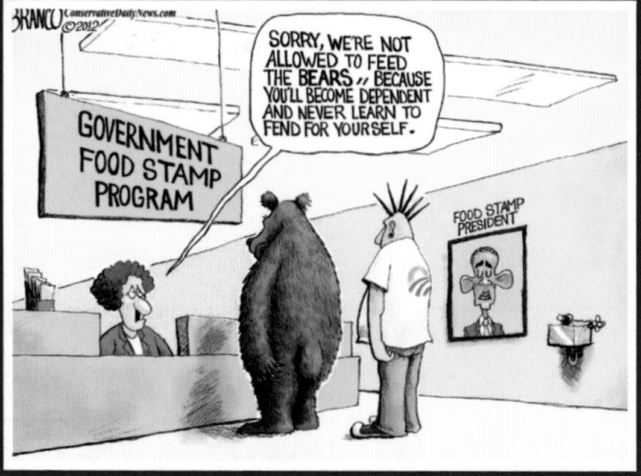
BRANCO ConservativeDailyNews.com ©2012
SORRY, WE'RE NOT ALLOWED TO FEED THE BEARS,, BECAUSE YOU'LL BECOME DEPENDENT AND NEVER LEARN TO FEND FOR YOURSELF.
GOVERNMENT FOOD STAMP PROGRAM
FOOD STAMP PRESIDENT

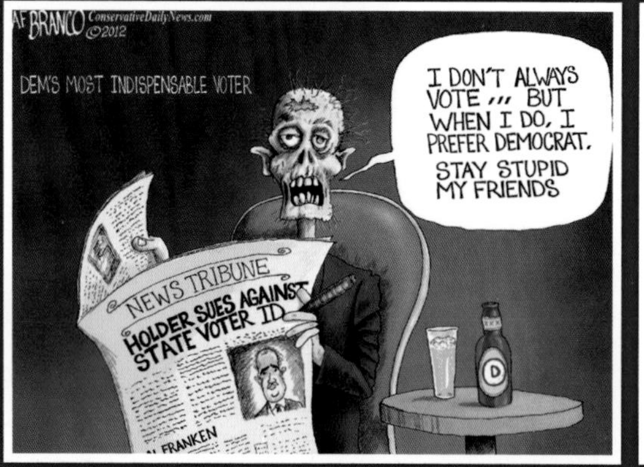
AF BRANCO ConservativeDailyNews.com ©2012
DEM'S MOST INDISPENSABLE VOTER
I DON'T ALWAYS VOTE,,, BUT WHEN I DO, I PREFER DEMOCRAT.
STAY STUPID MY FRIENDS
NEWS TRIBUNE
HOLDER SUES AGAINST STATE VOTER ID
AL FRANKEN
D

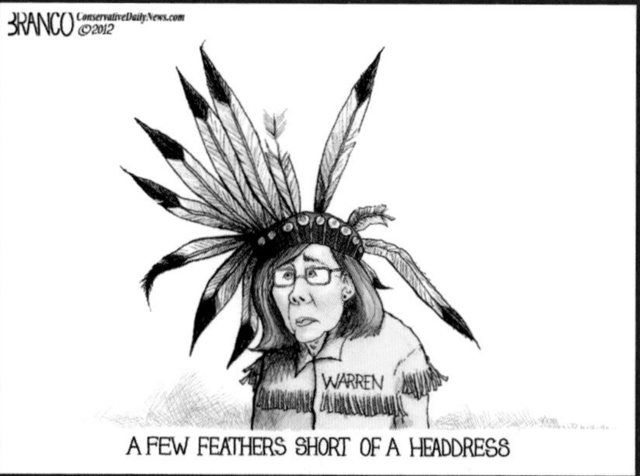
BRANCO ConservativeDailyNews.com ©2012
WARREN
A FEW FEATHERS SHORT OF A HEADDRESS

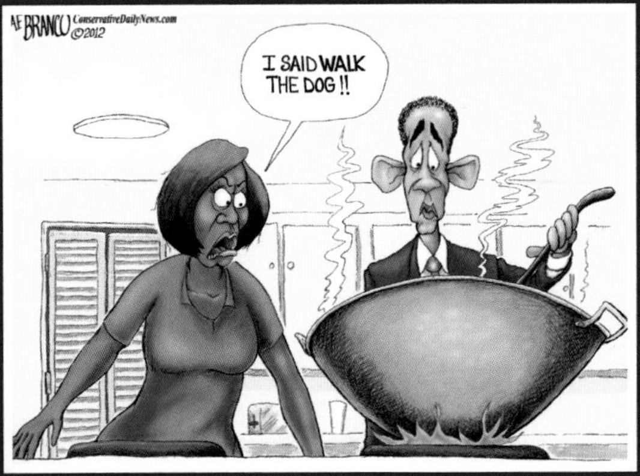

AF BRANCO ConservativeDailyNews.com ©2012
I SAID WALK THE DOG !!

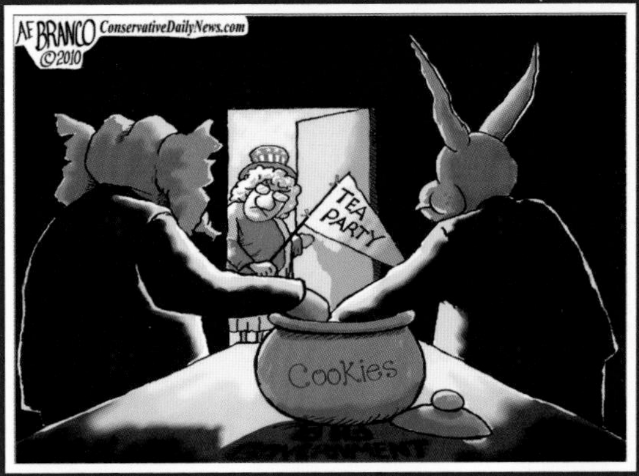

AF BRANCO ConservativeDailyNews.com ©2010
TEA PARTY
CooKies

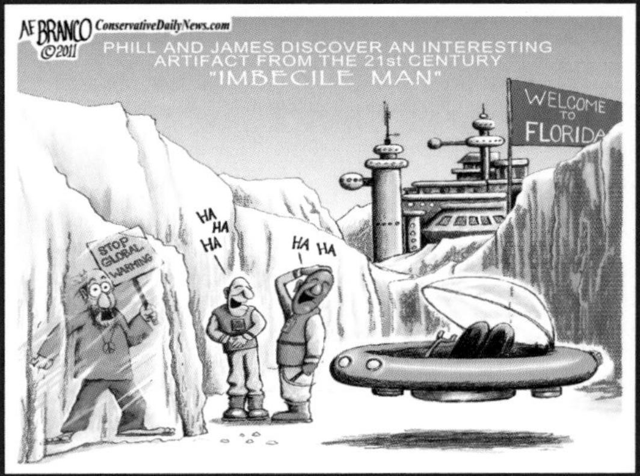

AF BRANCO ConservativeDailyNews.com ©2011
PHILL AND JAMES DISCOVER AN INTERESTING ARTIFACT FROM THE 21st CENTURY "IMBECILE MAN"
WELCOME TO FLORIDA
STOP GLOBAL WARMING
HA HA HA
HA HA

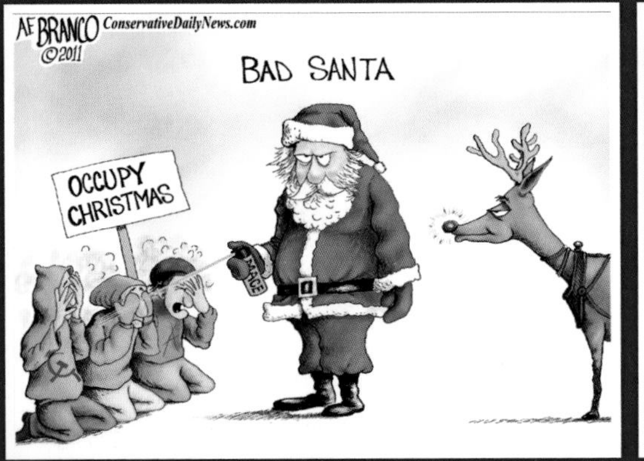

AF BRANCO ConservativeDailyNews.com ©2011
BAD SANTA
OCCUPY CHRISTMAS

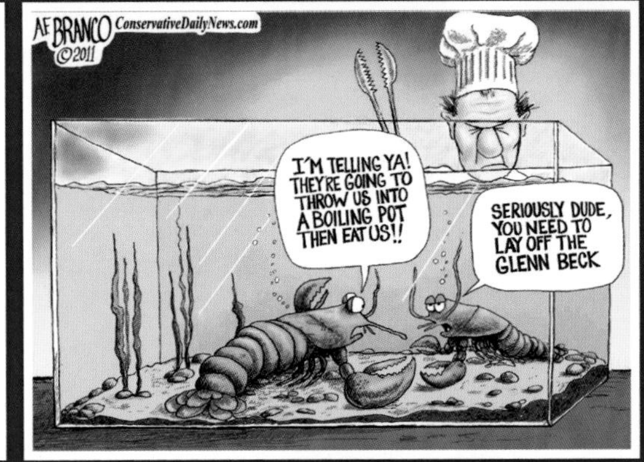

AF BRANCO ConservativeDailyNews.com ©2011
I'M TELLING YA! THEY'RE GOING TO THROW US INTO A BOILING POT THEN EAT US!!
SERIOUSLY DUDE, YOU NEED TO LAY OFF THE GLENN BECK

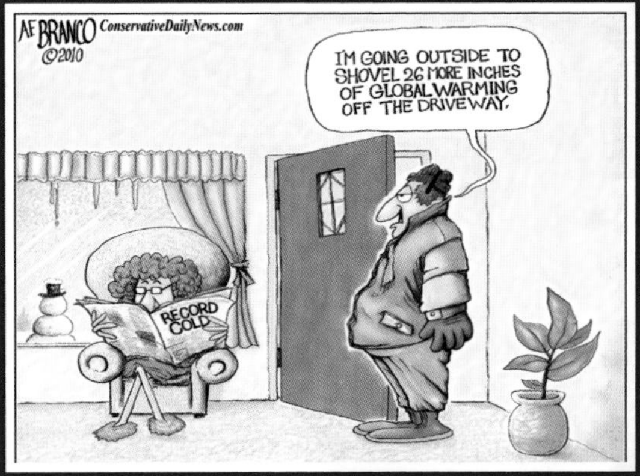

AF BRANCO ConservativeDailyNews.com ©2010
I'M GOING OUTSIDE TO SHOVEL 26 MORE INCHES OF GLOBAL WARMING OFF THE DRIVEWAY.
RECORD COLD

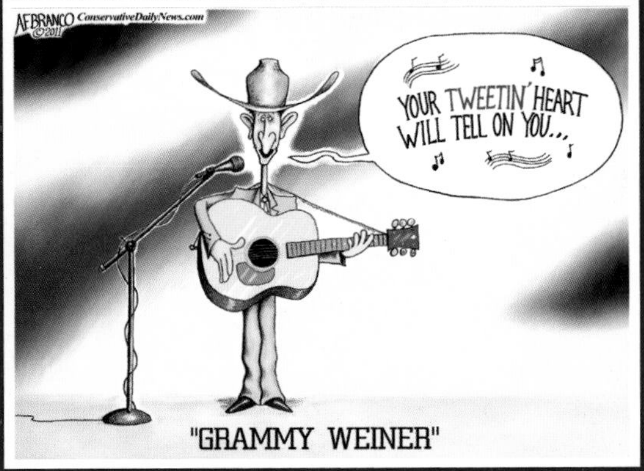

AF BRANCO ConservativeDailyNews.com ©2011
YOUR TWEETIN' HEART WILL TELL ON YOU...
"GRAMMY WEINER"

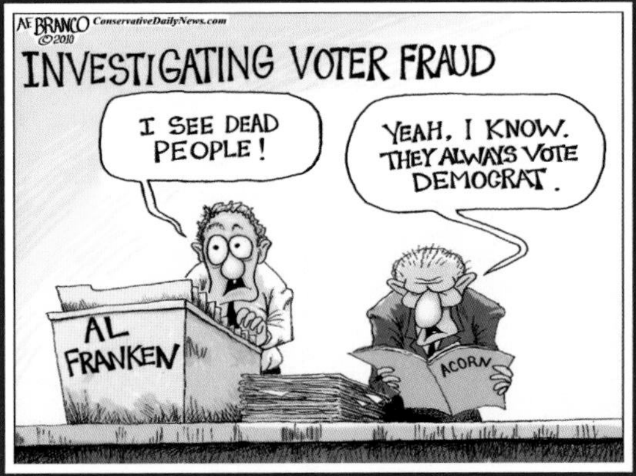

AF BRANCO ConservativeDailyNews.com ©2010
INVESTIGATING VOTER FRAUD
I SEE DEAD PEOPLE!
YEAH, I KNOW. THEY ALWAYS VOTE DEMOCRAT.
AL FRANKEN
ACORN

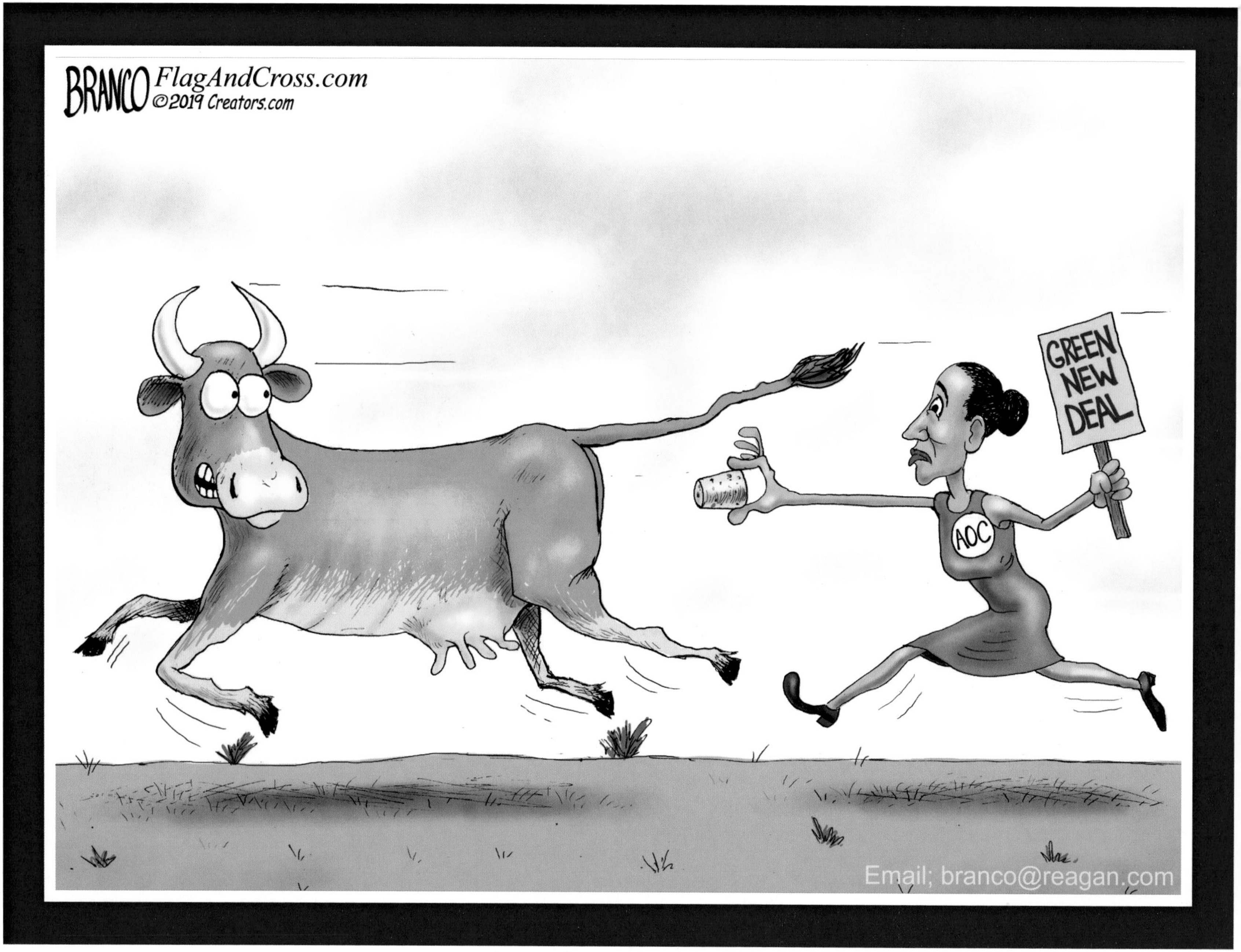
BRANCO FlagAndCross.com
©2019 Creators.com
GREEN NEW DEAL
AOC
Email; branco@reagan.com

The End